The Whole Spiel

May your matzah balls
always be floaters!.
Enjoy,

Ellen Scolnic   Joyce Eisenberg

The Whole Spiel

Funny essays about
digital nudniks, seder selfies
and chicken soup memories

ATM

$0 BUKES

say it in Yiddish

Joyce Eisenberg and Ellen Scolnic

Illustrations by Terry LaBan

Also by

JOYCE EISENBERG and ELLEN SCOLNIC

Dictionary of Jewish Words

(Jewish Publication Society 2001, 2006)

CONNECT ONLINE

www.thewordmavens.com

www.facebook.com/thewordmavens

twitter.com/thewordmavens

TERRY LaBAN

www.cartoonimpact.com

Published by
Incompra Press
414 South Olive Street • Media PA 19063
www.incomprapress.com

Paperback ISBN 978-0-692-72625-9
Library of Congress Control Number: 2016911742

Cover and text illustrations by Terry LaBan
Design and composition by Annette Murray

DEDICATION

To our grandparents, who spoke Yiddish when they didn't want the kids to understand what they were saying. This inspired us to find out what they were talking about.

The following essays first appeared, in a slightly different form and in some cases with different titles, in these publications:

The Philadelphia Inquirer:
"Swimming Safely in the Shallow End of the Technology Pool"
"Wanted: A Lamplighter, a Toll Taker and an Ice Man"
"No Question Unanswered: Google to the Rescue"
"Another Shopping Rewards Club? Count Us In"
"We Love the Tchotchkes of Christmas"
"Many Happy Returns"
"Sorting Through a Lifetime of Stuff"
"Our Kids Teach Us the Darndest Things"
"The Trouble With Digital Nudniks"
"It's Summertime and We Need to Rent a Kid"
"(Often) Lost & Found (Sometimes)"

The Forward:
"You Don't Know These Jewish Summer Holidays"
"Let My People Go Home Early"
"Two Chances to Ring in the New Year"
"You Say Wonton; We Say Kreplach"

InterfaithFamily.com:
"A Balabusta in Buckingham Palace?"

Contents

Introduction

We grew up hearing words like *kinder, chutzpah, shluff* and *shmutz*, and we thought they were part of a mysterious language reserved for grown-ups. They were, and that was the whole point. When our parents and grandparents didn't want us to understand what they were saying, they would speak to each other in Yiddish.

When Joyce was 6 years old, she spent the weekend with her cousins at Grandmom Sophie's house. She remembers feeling insulted when cousin Joe called her a name – he called her a bosom! – so she tattled on him. Joe defended himself. "Grandmom, I didn't call her a bosom; I called her *ongeblozzen*. You know, the word you always say."

While Joyce's grandmother had never explained to her that ongeblozzen meant sulky or pouty, Ellen's father never even told her that he spoke Yiddish. When she was a teenager she went on a family trip to Israel, and she was stunned when her father started talking to a cab driver in the only language they had in common – Yiddish.

In spite of the fact that our grandparents and parents didn't teach us the language, or perhaps because of it, we've been committed to expanding our Yiddish vocabulary. Although we aren't fluent, we can't help but sprinkle these beloved words into our conversations. When we text our kids to tell them that we're *kvelling* about their successes or refer to the bird poop on the windshield as shmutz, we know that our roots are firmly planted in 19th-century Eastern Europe, where Yiddish was king.

We love the Yiddish language – with its phonetically challenging adjectives and descriptive insults – and we pay attention when Yiddish makes an appearance in the media. Sometimes it's used correctly; at other times it's not. When the College of Cardinals met to choose a new Pope at the Vatican, reporters described their meetings not as "talking" or "discussing" but as *"shmoozing."* When U.S. Sen. Arlen Specter died, a columnist wrote, "He was imperious and difficult in a way that brilliant men can be. To use a Yiddish word, he had *shpilkes.*" We say, "The kids have shpilkes" (ants in their pants) when they're fidgety in the restaurant. The writer probably meant chutzpah.

We had chutzpah when we set out to write a practical, user-friendly guide to Hebrew, Yiddish and English words related to Judaism – even though neither one of us was fluent in Hebrew or Yiddish.

Since the Jewish Publication Society released our *Dictionary of Jewish Words*, we have moved on to writing personal essays together. Yes, this is an oxymoron. Personal means unique and individual, yet we often find ourselves writing about "the nice Jewish guy we're married to" or "our children" or "the time we burned our dinner."

How do we present our joint point of view without the reader assuming we're polygamists with five children between us? While we don't share husbands, we have shared paychecks, bylines and the microphone at our speaking engagements for the past 15 years. We write, blog, tweet and post as one, but we really are two people.

When we write together, we meld our points of view for the sake of the essay. So as not to embarrass a particular child, we disguise his or her identity. We use pronouns instead of names; add up all their ages, grade point averages and incomes; and divide by 5. Still, the kids recognize themselves. Both of our husbands thought we were talking about him when we wrote that "our husband" wanted to leave the wedding before the bride and groom had cut the cake. Likewise, when we described "our husband" as the nicest man in the world, they both said, "Thanks, sweetie."

In the time that we've been writing together, our children have gone from kindergarten to grad school, our phones have gone from our kitchen counters to our pockets, and our hair has gone from brown to needing a touch-up every six weeks.

Together we've written 1,400 definitions of Jewish words, 751 tweets, dozens of op-ed essays and 119 blog posts on topics ranging from *knipples* and *knishes* to year-round *shvitzing* and the crazy Jewish calendar. We kvell when an Indian boy spells *"knaidel"* correctly to win the National Spelling Bee, and we *kvetch* when the bagel store sells green bagels in honor of St. Patrick's Day.

We've spent hours and hours together driving to speaking engagements to talk about Jewish words with members of Sisterhoods and Men's Clubs, Hadassah and other groups. We love discussing what we've learned about Jewish families, traditions, holidays and foods – and the words that describe them.

Our audiences share with us their family memories, favorite recipes and the rituals that connect them to Judaism. They tell us funny stories:

One woman recounted that her son, who was in school in Kansas, walked into a drugstore before the Jewish New Year and asked the clerk for "a Rosh Hashanah card to send to my parents." The clerk replied, "We only stock Hallmark cards. They're in Aisle 1."

Another woman told us that her daughter, a third-grader who *shleps* a big backpack to school, lets out an *"oy"* when she lifts her bag out of the car each morning. One day the girl asked her, "Mom, what do people who aren't Jewish do when they need an oy?" That's a good question.

At our book talks, audience members always ask if we're working on a second book. What could be the follow-up to a dictionary? A thesaurus? A phone book? An encyclopedia? Well, for women like us who love to *shmooze*, simply defining a word isn't enough. Our follow-up is this book of essays because we not only want to give you the definition of *kine-ahora*, but we also need to tell you the whole *spiel* about how *bubbes* used to tie a ribbon to a baby's crib to keep the evil eye away.

Yiddish is the language many people think of when they say that a word or expression "sounds Jewish." In fact, the word Yiddish actually means "Jewish." Yiddish was first spoken about 1,000 years ago by French Jews who emigrated to towns along the Rhine River. To their vernacular, which was a combination of Hebrew and Old French, they added German words.

As Jews were expelled from Western Europe, they moved to Eastern Europe, carrying Yiddish with them and picking up new words from the local languages, including Russian, Polish and Ukrainian. For the Jews of the *shtetl*, Yiddish was the language of daily life; it was lovingly nicknamed the *mama loshen* (the mother tongue), and in the years preceding World War II, it's estimated than anywhere from six million to 11 million people spoke the language. That number was dramatically reduced by the Holocaust.

In the late 1800s, many Jewish immigrants shlepped across the Atlantic Ocean, bringing their Yiddish language with them. This was the height of Yiddish culture in America: *The Forward* was launched as a Yiddish language daily newspaper; it also printed the short stories and serialized the novels of Yiddish writers. New York City was home to almost two dozen Yiddish theaters and vaudeville houses.

As the years passed, the children of these new immigrants were eager to learn English and become Americans. They no longer wanted their language to keep them apart from mainstream America.

Today, Yiddish is enjoying a revival. College programs in Jewish studies are offering Yiddish language and literature courses. It's is being taught in adult ed classes and spoken in conversation groups at community centers. Comedians, sportscasters and newspaper editors turn to Yiddish when they need just the right word. We're happy to do our part, too.

Yiddish is written with Hebrew characters. Nearly one-fourth of all Yiddish words come almost unchanged from Hebrew, which is why the Hebrew and Yiddish versions of many words are similar. For example, "honor" is *kuvid* in Yiddish and *kavod* in Hebrew.

All of the Yiddish and Hebrew words in our essays are transliterated, which means we use English letters to represent the Hebrew characters. Since transliteration is based on how a word sounds, there's no one correct way to spell it. We chose *farklempt* instead of *verklempt* and *chutzpah* instead of *khutspe* because the former spellings are more common and we prefer them.

You'll often see Yiddish words spelled with "sch." We took our cue from Gene Bluestein, author of *Anglish/ Yinglish: Yiddish in American Life and Literature*, who wrote that spelling Yiddish words with "sch" is basically a German approach. In Yiddish, the "sch" sound is made by the Hebrew letter "shin," which means that the "sh" spelling is technically more correct. That's why we call the guy who forgets to put on a clean shirt before a date a *shlump*, not a *schlump*.

We have italicized Yiddish words on their first appearance in each essay and defined them in the Glossary at the end of the book. We have also italicized book, film and newspaper titles.

After you read our essays, we hope you'll invite your neighbor over for a *nosh* and a shmooze, tell the dog to stop being a *nudnik*, and thank your mom for being such a *balabusta*.

Acknowledgments

We are indebted to our Yiddish "teachers." At our book talks, we have met many *bubbes* who eagerly shared their memories of Shabbat dinners and told us how taking off their girdle is a *mechayeh*. We also met *zaydes* who raised their hands to tell us jokes with complicated Yiddish punch lines. For many years, Mitzi Eisenberg, Joyce's mother-in-law, was our go-to source for Yiddish definitions and classified bubbe information.

We were longtime fans of *Edge City*, the nationally syndicated comic strip about a hip Jewish-American family, and were delighted to connect with its creator, cartoonist Terry LaBan, who illustrated this book. He has *Yiddishkeit* and knew right away how to translate our 800-word essay about aging and missing our children into a hilarious cartoon of two middle-aged ladies playing miniature golf.

It's always great to have an editor who loves what you write. Our thanks to Kevin Ferris at *The Philadelphia Inquirer*, who finds space for our humor on his Commentary pages.

For years, the members of Playpen Writers Group, our friends and colleagues, have offered support, gentle critiques and insider knowledge on where to get published – over coffee and bagels.

Thanks to Stephanie Harper, Pearl Kouzi, Phyllis Sager and Robin Seeherman, who read early drafts of this manuscript and provided insight and feedback; to Libby Madarasz, who was an adept proofreader; and to Playpen member Karen Ivory, for her skillful evaluation of the final version of this book.

We're grateful to Annette Murray, of StickyEarth.com, who aptly calls herself a "book midwife." With her publishing and design expertise, Annette made our labor painless and helped us produce a beautiful "baby."

Though we write personal essays together, we wanted to acknowledge our families individually, not collectively.

For my husband, Ted, my *bashert*, and my children, Ben and Samantha, who bring joy, excitement, humor and purpose to my life. You inspire me to be a *balabusta*, help me when I'm *farblondjet*, and give me so many reasons to *kvell*. – **J.E.**

For David, who unfailingly and enthusiastically supports all my endeavors, and for my three greatest projects – Mike, Jessie and Andy – who "like" my articles online, text me their news and goings-on, and Snapchat me from around the world. – **E.S.**

Costco Shnorrers, Suburban Balabustas and Baby Pulkes

Thick Thighs or Chubby Pulkes: Everything's Cuter in Yiddish

To a *bubbe,* there's nothing better than a baby with plump thighs. The Yiddish word for thighs is *pulkes,* as in "There's no question she's getting enough to eat. Just look at her pulkes!" Pulkes can also refer to poultry. That's why at a family dinner you can usually count on Aunt Millie the Martyr to say, "Don't waste a slice of white meat on me. Give it to the children. I'll eat the pulkes."

We're pretty sure that pulke is the only Yiddish word that has made the transition from poultry to people because, frankly, nothing about poultry is cute. We don't envy turkey wattles. We hide them beneath turtlenecks or consider getting laser treatments to shrink them. We don't like gooseflesh when it's on our arms, and we know plenty of folks who don't like their beak. But baby pulkes are adorable. They're soft; they're squeezable. They even smell good.

You can buy a baby bib that brags, "I've got pulkes." These bibs don't come in adult sizes because at some point you've got to stop bragging about your chunky thighs. But when? When you start to walk? When you're old enough to read the words on your bib? When your pulkes rub together even though they're squeezed into Spanx? If we call our substantial woman-sized thighs pulkes, will they be cute once again?

A fitting word for our pulkes – and the rest of our body – is *zaftig*. Zaftig literally means "juicy or succulent." It refers to a full-bodied, voluptuous, well-rounded woman. We love this word. It sounds soft and lovable and so much kinder than "overweight." You want to hug someone who's zaftig, not elbow her over because she's hogging the armrest. Flemish painter Peter Paul Rubens had a soft spot for plus-size women, giving rise to the term Rubenesque, which describes the zaftig women who frolic in his paintings. He is not, however, responsible for the Reuben sandwich, which many Rubenesque women enjoy eating.

Yiddish also has colorful words for other body parts: head and shoulders, knees and toes, and many areas in between.

A child's head is a *keppe,* slang derived from the Yiddish word *kop,* or head. A bubbe might say, "Joshy, lay your keppe on my shoulder and *gai shluffen* (go to sleep)." Here's hoping that Joshy grows up to have a Yiddishe kop (a Jewish head), which means he'll be clever and smart. There's a Yiddish word to describe that, too: *Sekhel* means common sense, good judgment or using one's noodle, as in "Make sure you wear a helmet when you ride your scooter. Have a little sekhel."

On the front of the keppe is the *punim,* or face. *Shayna punim* (pretty face) is a term of endearment often uttered by grandparents as they pinch a grandchild's cheek. Sometimes they pinch a little too hard and leave a fingerprint on that precious punim. That's why the grandson in Rob Reiner's fractured fairy tale, *The Princess Bride,* pretended to be sick when his grandfather visited: He wanted to avoid the cheek-tweak.

Shnoz, a variation of the Yiddish word *noz* (nose), usually refers to a sizable proboscis. No one ever says, "Look at the dainty shnoz on her." We're old enough to remember Jimmy Durante, the Italian-American singer and comedian who referred to his oversized nose as a *shnozzola.* Perhaps he learned the word shnoz from Eddie Cantor, one of his Jewish buddies, when they hung out together in Hollywood. "The Shnozzola" became Durante's nickname and, along with his talent, it brought him fame and fortune.

Not everyone is happy with his or her shnoz. Rhino-plasties, the official term for nose jobs, were performed in ancient India as early as 800 B.C. We first heard about nose jobs in 1967 when Andrea missed three days of high school and returned to class with faint dark circles under her eyes and a new bobbed nose.

Pupik is Yiddish for navel or belly button. Like pulkes, this is a case where the Yiddish word is way cuter than the body part that it describes. A pupik is adorable and would never be loaded with lint. It probably wouldn't be pierced either.

Yiddish curses often involve terrible things happening to various body parts, and the pupik is not immune. One of the most famous is *"Zoll vaksen tsibiliss in zein pupik"* ("Onions should grow in his navel"). You might be immune from this curse if you have an outie belly button.

Behind the pupik are the *kishkas,* Yiddish slang for guts or intestines, as in "When the elevator lurched, I felt it in my kishkas," or "It took kishkas to stand up to him like that." If the word sounds familiar, it's because kishka is a food that you may have seen in the deli or in your bubbe's kitchen. This Jewish version of sausage, also called stuffed derma, is baked, sliced and eaten with mustard or gravy. You wouldn't find kishka on heart-healthy menus these days; it's gone to high cholesterol heaven. But we digress.

Tuchis, literally "underneath," is a crude word for the rear end or buttocks. *Tushee* is the wiped-clean version. Tushee is not as cute as booty, as clinical as buttocks or as vulgar as ass. In years past, when parents were still allowed to spank their kids – or at least threaten to – they might warn that a *"potch in tuchis,"* a slap on the behind, would come to those who misbehaved.

Yiddish has a number of words for penis – and johnson is not one of them. *Shlong* is the Yiddish word for snake. *Shmuck* is a vulgar term for a penis, and *shmeckel* is a small penis. Although shmuck is sometimes hurled as an insult, there's another side to the story. In German, the word means jewelry, which may explain why male genitalia are sometimes described as the "family jewels." This is good news to those whose last name is Shmuckler: It's likely that their ancestors were jewelers, not jerks.

Until recently, we knew only one Yiddish word that referred to a vagina, and it was *knish*, which seems to spring from the same class of nicknames as muffin and cookie. There had to be another word for female genitalia. To find it, we cornered some bubbes in a back room, closed the window, drew the curtains and shut the door. They whispered *"shmunda"* and *"shmundie"* as the-words-that-shall-not-be-mentioned. We needed confirmation and got it from writer Elissa Strauss, who grew up with the terms "knish and shmundie, all innocent sounding, neither clinical nor vulgar." She never heard these words outside her own home until she went to have her you-know-what waxed, and the sign outside the establishment read "Shmundie Central." Then she knew she was in the right place.

If you put all these body parts together, you get a whole little person: a *maideleh* (little girl), *mameleh* (little mama), *tateleh* (little papa), *boychik* (little boy), or *bubbeleh* (you guessed it).

By the way, you don't have to be a bubbe to be a bubbeleh. "Be a bubbeleh and pass us the cheese Danish, please."

～ 2 ～

Will the Real Yiddish Word Please Stand Up?

"**J**amie, hand me the spatula. I've got to flip the *latkes*," said Grandmom Minnie as they cooked together in the kitchen.

No wonder Jamie grew up thinking that spatula was a Yiddish word. Jamie knew spoon and fork but not spatula, so she assumed it was one of her *bubbe's* Yiddish words. We imagine that if an Italian grandmother asked a child for a colander so she could drain the spaghetti, that child might grow up thinking that colander was an Italian word.

Spatula is one of those words that tries really hard to worm its way into the Yiddish language. They've got the "sch" or the "chuuch" or the "fah," and they sound vaguely insulting. Don't be misled by the sound: A schnauzer is not a Yiddish dog.

These imposters can fool us, too. We were surprised when a non-Jewish friend told us she would need to "finagle time off from work" to have surgery. How did she know this Yiddish word? We were even more surprised to find out that although it rhymes with bagel, finagle isn't Yiddish.

Finagle has been traced to the British word "fainaigue," meaning to cheat or renege. Today finagle means finding a way to get what you want. Synonyms include wangle, wheedle, trick and persuade. We're talking more clever than dishonest, like when we call Macy's and finagle a refund of the $35 late fee. After all, our electronic payment was only a day late.

Students who get the wrong answer on their algebra homework should know about the Finagle Factor, a variable that can be inserted into a formula to make the answer come out right. We should use it when we balance our checkbooks. We just finagle the numbers the old-fashioned way – by crossing out our total and writing in the bank's balance.

Is traipse a Yiddish word? It sounds Yiddish but it's not, although an online dictionary lists *shlep*, a certified Yiddish word, as its synonym. Both mean to drag, plod or trudge along. Maybe people get confused because traipse sounds like *treif*, the Yiddish word for food that isn't kosher. These two words can only intersect in a sentence like this: "We traipsed all the way to Chinatown for an order of treif pork lo mein."

Cockamamie, an adjective meaning ridiculous, absurd or foolish, sure sounds like a Yiddish word. When Clint Eastwood, who played a Secret Service agent in the film *In the Line of Fire*, told his frightened younger partner that "quitting is a cockamamie idea," we were tickled that a non-member of the tribe had used a Yiddish word.

We were mistaken; cockamamie is also an imposter. The word comes from "decalcomanie," a combination of the French words for "tracing" and "mania." Decalcomania, the process of transferring designs to pottery or artwork, was popular in the mid-1800s. When the transfers were marketed to children as temporary tattoos in the 1940s, the name was changed to cockamamies because it was easier for children to pronounce. Today the word refers to any crazy idea, as in "My kid says he wants to go to Times Square on New Year's Eve. What a cockamamie idea!"

Svelte is not a Yiddish word, but we desperately wish it were. Svelte sounds tall, thin, blond and Swedish, but it actually comes from the French and means slim or slender. We shouldn't be surprised because those elegant French women are the ones who eat all that rich food and don't get fat. They stay svelte. We hate them. We are way more familiar with the Yiddish word *zaftig*, pleasingly plump.

French isn't the only language that offers up Yiddish pretenders. Kibosh, a word of unknown origin, seems like a first cousin to *kibitz*, the Yiddish word for joking around, but it's not. It's more like a cranky aunt: "Sid, put the kibosh on your kibitzing!"

"Gezellig," Dutch for "warm and cozy," and "zeg," the Georgian word for "the day after tomorrow," both sound very Jewish. "Come on *bubbeleh*, let's get gezellig and snuggle on the sofa. Oh, you're busy today? How about zeg?"

It's easy to get confused about what's what when there's little difference between a Yiddish word (*tummel*) and its English counterpart (tumult). Both words mean noise, ruckus or commotion, but when you're at a ballgame and the crowd is boisterous, you'd call it a tumult. At a Bar Mitzvah party, when the music gets too loud and the teens get too antsy, Jewish grandparents have been known to *kvetch*: "Too much tummel!"

Oprah Winfrey, the *maven* of popular culture, invented her own Yiddish word: *shlumpadinka*. She combined the Yiddish word *shlump* (a dull colorless person) with a made-up suffix, dinka. She used the word to describe shlumpy housewives who don't care how they look: They wear baggy sweatpants, leave home without makeup and gather their hair in a messy ponytail. Oprah did a makeover and turned a shlumpadinka into a superstar.

Oh Oprah, we couldn't finagle an invitation to appear on your show, but we did make up a Yiddish word, too: We grew up with mothers who preached the virtues of matching outfits. "If I'm going to buy you that plaid skirt, you better pick out a blouse that goes with it so you don't look *ongepotchket* (thrown together)," they'd say when they took us back-to-school shopping. These days, when our daughters throw together an outfit, they look chic. We call their style "prettypotchket."

～ 3 ～

It's Not Your Bubbe's Lingo

Back in the day, *shmutz* was really shmutzy. In the *shtetls* of Eastern Europe, cleaning up the shmutz meant dealing with horse manure, muddy boot prints and potato peels strewn on the wooden kitchen table. These days, we call it shmutz when we are sweeping up crushed Cheerios from the tiled kitchen floor.

Along with shmutz, many Yiddish words have made the transition to the 21st century. That's partly because *bubbes* have learned to send email and go online for recipes, but it's also because many of these evocative words don't have a counterpart in English.

Mechayeh is one of these words. In the shtetl, it was a mechayeh (a relief) when Russian soldiers on horseback rode by without stopping to break down your door. A century later, Bubbe calls it a mechayeh when she wriggles out of her tight girdle at the end of the day and when, on a hot summer day, she scoops up a handful of cool ocean water and pours it down the front of her bathing suit. We call it a mechayeh when we've been running errands all day long in the heat and our last stop is a store that's air-conditioned. When we slip off our high heels under the table at a wedding reception. When we take that first sip of fresh hot coffee in the morning.

When our parents talked about *shnorrers*, they meant moochers – the neighbor who asked to borrow a cup of sugar once a week or the uncle who grabbed the last three hors d'oeuvres at the wedding. When we talk about shnorrers, we mean the folks lurking by the free sample counters at Costco.

We feel a twinge of guilt when we grab the largest piece of chocolate chip cookie from the bakery's sample bowl with no intent to buy a pound, but are we shnorrers? Would a shnorrer feel remorse? This got us thinking: Are you a shnorrer if you . . .

- routinely toss the hotel's little shampoo and lotion bottles into your suitcase?
- take home the Sweet'N Low from the deli sugar bowl?
- say to your really hungry family, "Come on, that's us!" when the maître d' calls out an unintelligible name?
- continue to accept dinner invitations from the neighbors who had you over three times even though you've never reciprocated?

Maybe you are a shnorrer, unless you donate those hotel shampoos to a homeless shelter and slide a Sweet'N Low to your friend in the coffee shop. Then you're a hero.

Nosh is another Yiddish word that's used quite often, as in "What's with this restaurant menu and its small plates? They're no more than a nosh!"

Our grandparents' idea of a good nosh was pickled herring or a *shmeer* of chopped liver on rye. When we visited Bubbe, we preferred to nosh on her cookies: the *kichel* and the *kamishbrodt*.

In our homes, a nosh before dinner might be baby carrots dipped in hummus, a few pieces of sushi, or the chicken Caesar wrap left over from yesterday's lunch. We still call it a nosh, even if it's low-fat, low-salt and microwaveable.

Jewish delis are known for their noshes. Deli guys pass out free samples of pastrami or put a plate of toothpick-speared sour pickles on the deli counter so customers can help themselves. After that, who needs lunch? Free noshes are a shnorrer's dream.

Getting dressed up – all *fapitzed* – used to mean taking your mink coat out of storage as soon as there was a chill in the air. Wearing a dress and heels to get on an airplane. Getting your hair done on Friday and asking for extra hairspray so that it would hold for a week. Buying a new pair of stockings for Saturday night.

Fapitzed is not so fapitzy anymore. We're all about comfort, not style, so we fly in stretch pants and sneakers. If we can get away with wearing wide-leg fancy pants instead of a dress to a party, we do. We haven't worn pantyhose in years, but we're not alone. Even the best-dressed celebrities walk the red carpet at the Oscars with bare legs. Our mothers would disapprove.

In our homes, the last time anyone got all fapitzed was when our daughters were toddlers and we put them in ruffled dressy dresses or two-piece outfits adorned with sequined hearts. They stopped letting us dress them up decades ago, and now our girls dress up in a skirt made in India and a blouse that looked old when it was new.

There are so many funny-sounding Yiddish words that we could *plotz*. In fact, plotz is one of these words; it means to burst from excitement, pleasure or surprise. Plotzing is usually a good thing.

Bubbe plotzed when she won the Hadassah raffle for a free weekend at the fancy-shmancy Traymore Hotel in Atlantic City. She double-plotzed when her granddaughter called and said, "Bubbe, I want you to be the first to know that I'm getting engaged to Aaron Gold."

It's harder to plotz from surprise these days because everything is on Facebook. We know that you went to Aruba with your sister and brother-in-law. We saw the photos of your cute new puppy, and we watched the video of how your boyfriend proposed.

But we do plotz with excitement when our kids text us that they are unexpectedly in town and want to come by for dinner, and we plotz with pleasure when the whole family is together – all dressed up and dancing the hora – at cousin Danny's Bar Mitzvah.

Wikipedia has an entire page devoted to scandals, but our bubbes would call them *shandas*, the Yiddish word for shame or disgrace. Remember when that terrible Madoff man stole everyone's money? It was a shanda of the worst kind. How about when Elizabeth Taylor stole that nice Jewish boy Eddie Fisher from Debbie Reynolds back in 1958? That shanda even shocked Hedda Hopper, Hollywood's reigning gossip columnist.

Scandals aren't new: When Laban tricked Jacob into marrying Leah instead of Rachel, his true love, it was a shanda, but it was reported in the Bible, not the *National Enquirer*.

We *kvell* when newspaper reporters, TV anchors and comedians sprinkle some of our bubbes' lingo into their scripts. We're holding out hope that *pupik* (belly button), *gornisht* (nothing) and *ongeblozzen* (sulky) will make the headlines in the coming year.

∞

∽ 4 ∽

So Many Ways to Call Someone a Jerk

Just like Eskimos have dozens of words for snow, people who speak Yiddish have dozens of words to describe no-goodniks. The *shlemiels* and *shlimazels* just can't catch a break; they are nice guys, but they're not in the top 10 on JDate. Some never learned their manners: The *bulvan* is a coarse oaf; the *vilde chaya* is a wild beast. The *shlub* doesn't put on a clean shirt to go out to dinner, and the *shnook* doesn't know his head from a hole in the ground. The *shmeggegge* is an untalented loser; the *shmendrick* is an unimportant pipsqueak.

Why are there so many Yiddish words for lazy, foolish men? Here's our theory: Yiddish was the primary language of Ashkenazic Jews in the *shtetls* of Central and Eastern Europe, where a woman's work was never done. Housewives went to the market to buy potatoes and haggle over the price of chicken. Then they *shlepped* everything back home to transform meager ingredients into chicken soup, *kugel* and challah, the braided egg bread eaten on Jewish holidays and the Sabbath. They grated potatoes without a food processor, washed clothes without a Maytag, and killed and plucked their chickens instead of unwrapping a Styrofoam tray of boneless breasts.

We suspect that not many of their husbands, those shmendricks and shmeggegges, ever offered to set the table or take out the trash. When the men got home from a hard day at work as a peddler or cobbler, chances are they hung out with the guys – praying and studying Torah, the first five books of the Bible. They didn't watch basketball or play poker, but we assume they didn't help out around the house much either.

The women, who had a lot to *kvetch* about but little spare time to do it, depended on colorful Yiddish descriptions. Why say, "My Harold never asks for directions; he's as stubborn as a mule" when you could simply say, "My Harold is an *eyngeshparter*"? In the Old Country, it seemed that every day was April Fools' Day.

The Complete Idiot's Guide to Learning Yiddish lists more than 75 words for "the fools and villains of Jewish life" in its chapter on "Morons and Misfits." Though similar in meaning, these insulting nicknames are not interchangeable. Each has a distinct connotation, and it's easy to get all *farmisht* (confused) when you're trying to figure out who's who.

You don't hear many of these Yiddish words bandied about anymore, and that's a shame because they make us laugh. You're more likely to hear today's no-goodniks referred to as slackers, goof-offs, couch potatoes and deadbeats, but sometimes you just need a good Yiddish word, like these:

Luftmensch would be the perfect word for a guy who is addicted to Assassin's Creed and thinks his "skills" will get him a job designing video games. He is a dreamer with his head in the clouds.

When your teenage son plops down on the sofa after basketball practice and slips off his stinky sneakers, you could call him a *farshtinkener* (really smelly) boy.

When your friend adopts a rescue dog – a combination Chihuahua and German shepherd with a torn ear and mottled fur – you could describe the dog as a *mieskeit*, a little ugly thing, but you should keep it to yourself.

A *nebbish* is not necessarily a no-goodnik because yesterday's nebbish is today's nerd, and that nerd could be the millionaire owner of a software company or the star of a hit TV show. On the other hand, *yutz* has not gotten a makeover; it still describes a hapless, clueless, socially clumsy guy. "Please don't fix me up with Stanley. I went out with that yutz last year, and once was quite enough!"

Both *putz* and *shmuck* literally mean "penis," but while a putz is a fool or a jerk, a shmuck is an obnoxious or detestable person. You would think that only a *grober yung* (a coarse young man) would use such vulgar words, but you'd be wrong. Hollywood offers up plenty of examples. The action comedy *Ishtar* is remembered as a terrible film with one great scene: when Dustin Hoffman teaches Warren Beatty how to pronounce "shmuck." When *Dinner for Schmucks* premiered in 2010, the word shmuck went from actors' mouths to movie theater marquees.

Shmo, a shortened, sanitized version of shmuck, refers to a boob or a jerk. We can live with a shmo, and that's good news because you can find a Joe Shmo anywhere. He's a Jewish John Q. Public, the man on the street, the common man: "Don't stop for coffee today. They are giving away free donuts. It'll be busy with Joe Shmos."

You won't encounter a Janis Shmo. That's because there aren't many Yiddish words for female no-goodniks. You could call us *yentas* (gossipy blabbermouths) or *yachnes* (malicious gossipy blabbermouths), but we'd prefer *balabustas*, literally "mistresses of the house," high praise for women who can cook, bake, launder and keep the house spotless, as in "She has three kids and no help in the house, and she's hosting a holiday dinner for 22 people. She's a real balabusta."

Friend Us on
'the Facebook'

～5～

Swimming Safely in the Shallow End of the Technology Pool

Every now and then, we find ourselves asking questions that prove we're not as hip or with it as we think we are. And undoubtedly, when our kids read this, they'll tell us that nobody says "hip" or "with it" anymore.

We love new apps, gadgets and conveniences, and we marvel at the things they can do, but we don't fully trust them. We spent decades dialing the phone, putting family photos in albums, and getting up from the chair to change the channel. No wonder "swiping," "clicking" and "streaming" can sometimes confuse us.

If we still don't understand how Adele's big new song can travel from England and come out of our tiny clock radio, how can we possibly comprehend how money can fly wirelessly through the air from our bank account into yours?

We're most familiar with the old-fashioned ways of taking care of business. We remember smudging our fingers when we used carbon paper, sniffing the freshly mimeographed quizzes in grade school, and dipping the tiny brush into the bottle of Wite-Out, which got crusty and dried out before it was used up.

So even though we use modern technology, we sometimes talk about it in outdated terms. Here are some questions that don't need to be asked anymore, but we just can't help ourselves:

Do you need directions to my house? That's what we asked the painter when he called to set up a time to meet. We forgot that he's probably been using Google Maps on his smartphone for years. He can even navigate around a traffic jam, change his route to the one that's "two minutes faster," or look at a street view of our house before he arrives. We use Google Maps too, but we still keep that torn, awkwardly folded map of Pennsylvania in the glove compartment as a backup.

Did you get the message we left on your answering machine? What we actually did was leave a voicemail on our friend's cellphone. She doesn't even have an answering machine. With her cellphone, our friend can retrieve our message while standing in line at the pet store; she doesn't have to wait until she gets home to her kitchen. One of us still has an answering machine hooked up to her landline phone; if the light is blinking once a month, it's cause for excitement.

Do you have a deposit slip for that check? We transfer money between our accounts electronically, and we've used ATMs all over the world, but we still write and deposit the occasional paper check. Handing it to the teller is the only way we can be certain that it will go into our account. When one of our children asked about the easiest way to deposit a paycheck, we handed her a deposit slip. She ignored us, Googled "how to put money in the bank," downloaded the bank app and took a photo of her check.

Our 20-something daughter paid her share of lunch by using the Venmo app to send $8.50 to her girlfriend. When we go out to lunch, we each put a $20 bill on the table and ask the waiter to bring us change in singles so we can leave a tip.

Did you print out your train ticket? We can't help but ask our kids this question before they head off on a journey. They explain that their eTicket is on their phone; they'll just show it to the conductor. When we travel, we print out the confirmation and also scrawl "AF383C" on a scrap of paper. We print out our concert tickets and hotel reservations. It's easier for us to find a piece of paper in our purse than to locate that one confirmation email – among the 462 we haven't deleted – on our phone.

Did you write down your password? One of our sons was alarmed that we keep a small address book filled with screen names and passwords on the desk alongside the computer. "There's an app for that," he told us. But what if our phone is dead? How will we get to the app? We keep a spare copy of our passwords in a Word document on the computer, but what if the power goes out? That's why we have to write it in the little book.

Sometimes it's not our words but our hand gestures that give us away. Scribbling in the air is the universal sign to ask for the check, but when one of our husbands swirled his index finger in a circle as he said, "I'll call you," he dated himself. To him, making a call involved putting his index finger in the corresponding hole on the phone and rotating clockwise seven times. His childhood phone number started with letters – GR for Greenwood – but he can't call it anymore.

Our adult children are totally immersed in technology. They grew up with it so they have no other frame of reference. We had to explain to them that once upon a time you had to walk over to the TV to change the channel, that when you made a typo on your homework it was on the page forever, and that "a quarter to seven" is 6:45.

We think of modern technology like a swimming pool: We're all having a great time, but while our kids are frolicking in the deep end we're wearing swimmies and hanging on the rope – just in case.

∽ 6 ∽

Wanted: A Lamplighter, a Toll Taker and an Ice Man

Where have all the copy boys gone? What about the lamplighters, elevator operators and bowling alley pinsetters? They are nowhere to be found.

Neither is the operator at Directory Assistance, who used to look through her Yellow Pages to find the phone number of Gimbels department store. When Gimbels was in its heyday, it had a busy hat department stocked with pillbox hats, straw hats and felt cloche hats. Nowadays, you can count the number of milliners on the fingers of your kid-gloved hands. After all, when was the last time you bought a custom-made hat?

Recently, a dead landline had us looking for a telephone repairman, so we blew the dust off our Yellow Pages and flipped to "Small Appliance Repair," only to discover that the independent telephone repairman is extinct. Why would he repair the phone when a new, corded model sells for $14.99 at Target?

The butcher, the baker and the candlestick maker are disappearing, too. Instead, you can buy filet mignon from the Omaha Steaks website, pick up red velvet cupcakes from the gourmet cupcake truck when it tweets its location, and order handmade soy candles online from Etsy.

You cannot, however, get your hair cut online, which is why hands-on service providers, such as hairstylists, manicurists and massage therapists, are still around. They actually have to talk to and touch their customers. Patty, the colorist at Curlz, will never be replaced by a robot.

Jobs change with the times. Nowadays they are called careers. With his horse-drawn wagon, Grandpop Henry delivered blocks of ice for kitchen iceboxes. Years later, he switched to a gasoline-powered truck and joined the Teamsters. Today, his grandson moonlights as an Uber driver, picking up customers who summon him with a swipe of their phone app.

As our kids wander down their own career paths, we find it hard to give them advice. Although we know what it takes to become a doctor or an accountant, we don't know what skills one needs to become a distance learning manager, luxury brand consultant, or corporate sponsor facilitator.

When she was filling out a form online, a 20-something friend had to scroll down to select her occupation. She fully expected that "holistic life coach" would be one of the choices on the drop-down menu. The list included traditional occupations, such as fisherman, oil rig worker and geologist, and hadn't been updated in decades. She had to settle for "other."

We find it especially hard to wrap our heads around jobs in the tech sector. We finally understand that a search engine optimizer is the person Frank calls to make sure that "Frank's Honest Auto Repair" is the first name to pop up when you Google "fix my car," but what's on the to-do list of a cloud architect or mobile app manager?

We do know what's on the agenda of a professional pooper-scooper, and we don't want to do it. It's one of the many tasks that people used to do themselves and are now outsourcing – but not to India. Pet owners can also avail themselves of dog walkers and canine behaviorists.

Parents can turn to baby-proofing technicians, camp consultants, and college financial aid navigators. They'll be lucky if they don't need the services of professional nitpickers when head lice spread through the third grade.

Along with tech and personal-service jobs, green jobs are on the upswing. We're all in favor of going green. We recycle. We carry a reusable water bottle, and we turn off the tap when we brush our teeth. We have instituted all these measures without the help of a corporate sustainability manager, recycling coordinator or solar power expert.

We're old enough to remember when "cutting and pasting" involved an X-Acto knife and glue and when we couldn't plan a trip without a travel agent. So when we exit the turnpike, we'll choose the E-ZPass lane and salute the one remaining toll taker as we zoom by. Her job is on the endangered list.

∽ 7 ∽

No Question Unanswered: Google to the Rescue

After Hanukkah, one of us turned to Google to find out "how to get wax off a menorah." She went with the result that advised "freeze the menorah and the wax pops right off." It did, but so did the decorative tiles that her daughter had so carefully glued to the candleholder years ago in preschool.

She needed some glue to reattach the tiles and soon was Googling "fingersstucktogether with Krazy Glue." She took the advice to use nail polish remover. Her next search was "how to repair acetone-damaged wood table."

Had she gone old school and used a butter knife to scrape off the wax, she would have been searching the medicine cabinet for a Band-Aid instead.

This recent Googling spree inspired us to analyze our online search behavior. Most often, we're simply curious: Wasn't Benedict Cumberbatch the villain in the recent

Star Trek movie? When was the song "Girls Just Want to Have Fun" on the charts? Thirty years ago? Really?

In the old days, we would have had to go to the library to get these questions answered, but we wouldn't have cared enough to make the trip. Growing up, we remember the set of encyclopedias that made the den bookshelf buckle. When we asked our parents a question, they would order us to "Go look it up!"

Now we can look up anything on our smartphones – from the real name of the artist formerly known as Prince to the names of the countries formerly known as Yugoslavia – and get an answer in seconds.

At other times, we Google for a reason:

To not look stupid: During the Krazy Glue mishap, we could have called a doctor for advice, but that would mean admitting our carelessness. Besides, who can call with three fingers stuck together?

For parenting advice: What do you do when your kid has a meltdown in a restaurant? Should you let your child binge-watch *Peppa Pig*? Googling gives modern moms an advantage; they can ask a question and get loads of advice without risking embarrassment. Our kids' formative years were mostly pre-internet. We had to ask fellow moms in the playground if it was normal for a 4-year-old to throw a screaming fit in the supermarket checkout line. Now our kids are grown, so we ask Google, "What are the job prospects for recent grads with a liberal arts degree?" and "When should you meet his girlfriend's parents?"

To win an argument: This works best in one-on-one situations. If you search hard enough, you can always find someone online who agrees with you – yes, bright orange is a soothing color to paint the bedroom. Googling is especially useful when you are trying to prove that your fabricated Scrabble word is valid. No, it's not a real word just because it can be found in someone's unedited blog. Google is no match for Noah Webster.

If you are arguing publicly whether the Eagles have won more Super Bowls than the Jets, someone will invariably whip out a phone and offer to look it up for you. The old days of "You owe me five bucks" are gone. Thanks to Google, you'll know who's right before you have time to make a pinky bet.

To prevent food poisoning: We used to just make snap judgments when it came to expiration dates. Chopped liver? If you have to ask, it's been too long. Yogurt that expired five days ago? It's filled with bacteria anyway. It probably can't hurt us.

Now we let the internet be our judge. Googling "Is this eggplant rotten?" led us to YouTube videos of self-professed experts. After four minutes of watching a young woman run her hand down the surface of the eggplant and talk about its firm skin, we still didn't have an answer, so we tossed the eggplant out. What about the five-day-old chili in the back of the refrigerator? An online guide to shelf life gave us permission to eat it. We didn't get a stomachache, so we consider it to be a reputable source.

For sage advice: If our grandmothers were alive, we'd call them to find out how to prevent matzah balls from sinking to the bottom of the bowl of chicken soup and how they managed to stay happily married for 55 years. Even though Google served up 3,490 results for "floater matzah balls" and plenty of hints on "ways to keep the spark alive," we decided that it is no substitute for Grandmom.

To hide our failing memories: Asking our kids for the millionth time, "What's the name of the street we turn left on to get to your new apartment?" only gets us an annoyed sigh. We know our aging brains are turning into sieves, so we turn to Google for nonjudgmental answers.

Google Maps is happy to tell us, over and over again, that the street is Bridlewood Drive.

When we can't find our cellphone for the millionth time, we call it from our landline. If we don't hear it ring, we don't know whether the battery is dead or the phone is under the driver's seat in the car. We'd like to use the handy Find My iPhone app, but we can't remember how it works. So we search for "how to use Find My iPhone," and Google gives us the five easy steps.

For permission: We're excited to go to a friend's birthday party this weekend, but we don't know if the "red bumpy rash on my arm" is contagious. We Google it and learn that it could be anything from eczema (not contagious) to African flea fever (not likely). We go to the party. If we're still rashy in a week, we'll call the doctor.

When it comes to getting useful information, Google is our favorite. Siri doesn't understand us. Cortana plays hard to get. That's why when we need an honest opinion, we simply Google "Does this dress make me look fat?"

⌐ 8 ⌐

Another Shopping Rewards Club? Count Us In

As we waited in the airport for a flight back to Philadelphia, we glanced at our boarding passes and were pleasantly surprised to see Group 1 printed at the bottom. Group 1? We are usually in Group 4, along with the woman who forgot she had a 24-ounce bottle of shampoo in her purse.

When the agent announced that the plane was ready for priority boarding, we got up from the plastic seats, ready to go. Then he welcomed those seated in first class.

Then families with small children were "welcome to board."

Then, "any uniformed members of the Armed Forces." That seemed fair.

We moved toward the front. Group 1 had to be next.

Then he called for "all members of the Admirals Club, the Advantage Club and those with elite status: the diamond, ruby and emerald credit card holders."

What credit card did we buy these plane tickets with?

By the time all the "special people" had boarded, we were left standing alone. Turns out that Group 1 wasn't very special after all.

We don't recall even being invited to join the Elite Diamond Club.

Many other clubs do want us as members, and not a day goes by without them emailing us with offers of bonus points, free food, rewards and advantages. Sometimes the advantages are dubious, but if you ask us, we'll likely sign up. We once stood in line to try a cronut and found ourselves signing up for the Delicious Cronut Loyalty Club just in case we ever had the urge to spend $5 again on a trendy iced pastry in a city we rarely visited.

When the clerk in the frozen yogurt store looked at our cups overflowing with Oreo cookie crumbs and wet walnuts, she asked, "Do you want to join our Frequent Eater Yummy Yogurt Club?" We couldn't resist. We were hoping that the next time we flipped the handle to start the flow of mint chocolate chip, she'd announce: "All members of the super secret Yummy Yogurt Club get free jimmies today."

We couldn't resist joining the Shmeer Society at the local bagel store either. But didn't they used to give you a free bagel when you bought a dozen without making you join their club?

Between us, we now belong to about two dozen loyalty programs. That's a lot of loyalty.

We can remember a time when we guarded our privacy, reluctant to divulge our email addresses and phone numbers to strangers. But now that we – and everyone else on the planet – can see the front of our houses on Google Maps, we know that keeping our details private is a lost cause. Privacy is a pipe dream, and registering for all of these rewards clubs doesn't help.

At the drugstore, the employee at the register prods us to enter our Plenti rewards program number before she'll even think about ringing up our greeting cards and Q-tips. "You get points and some money off," she chirps happily every time. We do as we're told, but invariably we get Plenti of nothin'. At the competing chain, our reward is a coupon for $4 off – next week. Since we just bought $45 worth of cold medicine, it's unlikely we'll need to come back in time to use that coupon. It'll expire on the floor of our car.

We do like our supermarket loyalty program, which provides instant gratification. After we rack up hundreds of dollars in groceries, we scan our super shopper card and watch the discounts pile up. Blueberries: minus $2.50. English muffins: minus 50 cents. At the end of the receipt is the proof: We saved $16.76. Woo-hoo! This will cover our impulse purchases of caramel sea salt gelato and organic cucumber face wash.

Even though the club cards clutter up our wallets, we prefer them to clipping coupons and then searching for each item in the store. We never mastered the art of extreme couponing. We've downloaded some reward apps that promise to keep track of what we eat and what we earn, but it's hard to remember our user names and passwords. When we do log on, we have to swipe through five screens to choose our salad ingredients and get credit for our purchase.

What do these loyalty clubs get us? When a friend wanted to get an appointment with a world-famous gastroenterologist within a week, her membership in the Rita's Water Ice Cool Customer Club didn't impress the receptionist enough to get her in to see the doctor.

If only our friend had been a member of the Elite Diamond Club. Surely that would have impressed the receptionist!

The Jewish Holidays: Let's Party Like It's 5777

∽ 9 ∽

You Don't Know These Jewish Summer Holidays

Sadly, there is a shortage of Jewish holidays between Shavuot, in late spring, when Moses received the Ten Commandments, and Rosh Hashanah, in early fall, when we celebrate the Jewish New Year.

Sure, there's Tisha b'Av, but who wants to throw a party on a day you are supposed to fast? Tu b'Av, the Israeli Valentine's Day, follows soon after, but we don't celebrate because it's hard to find a shmaltzy greeting card and chocolates that haven't melted in the summer heat.

We Jews like having a holiday to celebrate every few weeks or so. It gives us an excuse to get together, *shmooze* and eat. And while we love the Fourth of July, kosher hot dogs and fireworks do not a Jewish holiday make.

In the name of anthropological research, we dug into the vault and uncovered six little-known Jewish holidays. Won't you join us in celebrating this summer? We'll whip up an apple cake and set the table for 10.

Rosh To Barbecue

This festival of first fruits – and steaks and hot dogs – celebrates the first evening you light the barbecue and decide it's warm enough to eat dinner on the deck. Preparations for this holiday include scraping last year's *shmutz* off the grill, sending someone to get the propane tank filled, and stocking up on paper plates. Guests may come bringing offerings of pasta salad and fruit pie. Although a menorah is not necessary, it is customary to kindle the citronella lights. Celebrating this holiday requires you to remain outdoors even if everyone is freezing cold and shivering as the sun goes down. Every 17 years, the ritual of the "swatting of the mosquitoes" is replaced by the "crunching of the dead cicadas." On these years, read the alternative section in red in your prayerbook.

Pulke Day

This is the day when your *pulkes*, which are large and white and dimpled like chicken thighs, make a public appearance for the first time in the season. It corresponds with an invitation to your neighbor's backyard pool. This little-known day of mourning is primarily observed by women ages 45 to 65. Some choose to fast on this day, but it won't help. Neither will tanning. Later in the summer, even when your thighs are nice and tan, they will still be large and dimpled.

Yom Lo Kinder

Similar to Passover, this freedom festival is celebrated mainly by parents of children ages 6 to 16 on the day they drop the kids off at summer camp. While the children's holiday attire is informal, Jewish custom dictates that every article of clothing must be labeled with the name of the child. There is no special prayerbook for this holiday; prayers are spontaneous. The most frequently recited ones include the "Don't get sick so I have to come and fetch you" and the "Stop being homesick; you're not missing anything."

Emotions run high as parents are relieved, guilty, happy and sad to entrust their precious offspring into the care of inexperienced junior counselors. When the parents return home to an empty house, the ritual four cups of wine – the good stuff, not the sweet stuff – are often part of their celebratory meal.

Kine-a-Shnorrer

Celebrated by Jews who are fortunate enough to have a backyard swimming pool, this holiday ushers in the season when uninvited guests, the "summer ushpizin," drop by for "just a little swim." Those who observe this holiday year after year are familiar with the rituals: Guests swim, then ask for a little *nosh*, then you have to serve iced tea and offer them a dry towel. Before you know it, you're making sandwiches and have 10 loads of laundry to do. The Kine-a-Shnorrer holiday gives rise to the well-known expression "make a fence around the pool."

Shlepping Sand

This obscure pilgrimage festival is celebrated by Jews who live near a beach. This is the day when Jewish families load up the car with bikes, coolers and beach towels and journey to the sea. Although no temple sacrifice is necessary, parents do sacrifice sanity, money and personal space by sharing a rental house with the whole *mishpuchah*, the extended family.

At the conclusion of the Shlepping Sand festival, after loads of sand have been accidentally *shlepped* back home in crusty towels and unwashed beach toys, children begin the solemn "counting of the school supplies ritual," marking time until the first day of school. Traditional holiday foods include salt water taffy, Good Humor popsicles and squished tuna fish sandwiches. "Yes, they're still good. I packed them this morning."

Simchat Squash

This harvest festival is celebrated mainly by suburban Jews as they gather in the bounty from their 3-by-5 backyard plots. Offerings include black-spotted tomatoes, misshapen carrots, scraggly string beans and a plethora of zucchini. Customs include looking up zucchini recipes and recalling the legend in which God tells the Israelites, "Just eat it. It's good for you." Festive foods pay homage to the summer squash and include zucchini muffins, zucchini pancakes, zucchini bread and zucchini *kugel*. City-dwelling Jewish hipsters don't celebrate this holiday; they belong to food co-ops and community-supported agriculture programs (CSAs) and have to eat whatever veggies are in their weekly share.

～ 10 ～

Let My People Go Home Early

When we were growing up, our Passover seders were traditional. We kids would hide behind our Maxwell House haggadot, hoping *Zayde* wouldn't call on us to read the really long passage with the unfamiliar words. We didn't dare sneak a piece of matzah. It seemed like the seder dinner went on until midnight. Then there were all those songs with the crazy verses sung to age-old melodies at the end.

Nowadays, we are the hosts, and we get to make the rules. As Yul Brynner, the most famous pharaoh, said, "So let it be written; so let it be done."

Here are some ways our Passover seder will be different from all other seders this year.

Choosing which version of the haggadah, the small book of Passover prayers, songs and rituals, to use at the seder is a daunting task because thousands have been published and each is different. When the revered Jewish scholar Rashi put together his edition in the 11th century, he included the song "Dayenu" but left out "Had Gadya." The 14th-century *Sarajevo Haggadah,* a famous Sephardic manuscript, was handwritten on calfskin and illuminated in copper and gold. New haggadot are published every year.

There's even an updated edition of the Maxwell House haggadah, which more than 50 million people have used since it was first printed in the 1930s. This haggadah giveaway – you got a free copy when you bought a can of coffee – is considered the longest-running sales promotion in advertising history. On the inside cover it asks three important religious questions: Master Blend or Original Roast? Decaf or caf? Perk or drip?

We could use the "green" haggadah that adds air pollution and deforestation to the list of plagues or the feminist haggadah that focuses on the contributions of Miriam, Sarah, Rachel and other women in Jewish history. The hip-hop haggadah caters to those who want their Jewish tunes written by rap artists, while the *30 Minute Seder* haggadah accommodates guests who want to nibble the gefilte fish sooner rather than later.

While we're all in favor of diversity, we prefer to stick with the haggadah we pieced together through the years. We copied pages with our favorite passages, added contemporary rituals and catchy songs from preschool, and deleted the parts we didn't like.

When we recite the blessing over the first cup of wine, it's traditional to recline as royalty did in ancient times. After all, "now we are free" to slouch, even though we are sitting not on a throne but on a dusty folding chair that was *shlepped* up from the basement. We'll pass out pillows and tell everyone to lean any way they want. We're pretty sure that our nephew who goes to Oberlin will lean to the left, while Uncle Murray, who voted for George W., will tilt to the right.

After we ask the official Four Questions, we will raise a few more:

1. Who told Uncle Harry he could bring his new lady friend to the seder?
2. Why does a box of brownie mix that's kosher for Passover cost $8.19 when Duncan Hines sells for $3.99?
3. How many times should we refill the teens' wine glasses? They've had enough Manischewitz already.
4. Why do we gain weight on Passover when the food is so bad?

When we get to the part where we retell the story of the Israelites' exodus from Egypt and the kids grab costumes and masks, you'll know our seder is one where the macaroons will be passed around before 8:30. Ours is not the kind of seder where you are handed a 10-page script and a bongo drum and told, "Your part is Shifra, the midwife." That would be the beginning of a very long night.

A passage in the haggadah describes four children: the wise one, the wicked one, the simple one, and the one who does not know how to ask a question. We have always disliked this name-calling, and experts warn us not to label our kids. But last year when we looked around the table, we thought there might be something to this old rabbinic parable after all: One child was Googling to find out what animal a shank bone comes from. Another was texting a friend that our matzah balls were sinkers. The youngest was posting selfies from the seder, and Danny wasn't asking any questions; he had his headphones on.

When the haggadah instructs us to taste the maror, the bitter herbs, we will not ask our guests to share a bitter moment from their lives, as the authors of *Make Your Own Passover Seder* suggest. Asking guests to talk about the end of a relationship, loss of a job or other bad experience sounds like an idea from *The Buzz-Kill Haggadah* to us.

We've been known to change the date of Hanukkah to make it coincide with our kids' college breaks, and we're not afraid to change things up on the seder plate. We substituted a chicken bone for a lamb shank when the supermarket ran out. We once replaced the roasted egg with a plastic egg from the kids' play kitchen, but we've never gone vegan and replaced it with a small white eggplant like *The Vegan Haggadah* recommends. The sixth spot on the seder plate is reserved for hazeret, an additional bitter herb. We don't need more bitter. Instead, we'll fill this spot with a bridge toll receipt, symbolic of the many rivers our family and friends drove across to get to the seder at our house.

We always serve an Ashkenazic version of haroset – with chopped apples, nuts and sweet red wine – to symbolize the mortar the Israelites used to make bricks for the pyramids. This year we'll also include a Sephardic version made with dates, pistachios and cardamom, but we will not include the Sephardic ritual of dipping our fingers into that haroset and marking the doorway with a wine-soaked handprint so the Angel of Death will "pass over."

Everyone looks forward to the first bite of matzah. After a year of enjoying crusty, fluffy rolls, the unleavened flat cracker that's eaten during Passover seems tempting, but it gets old quick – long before the other four boxes in the "family pack" get eaten. The kids look forward to finding the afikoman, the piece of matzah that's hidden during the seder. We break the afikoman into multiple pieces so no child is a loser when the prizes are given out. This year we'll ask one of the kids to download the Find My Afikoman app so that an undiscovered piece of matzah isn't left in the piano bench for eight months. Not that this has ever happened in our homes.

We've always invited Elijah to our seder. In recent years, we've extended an invitation to Miriam, Moses' sister. In her honor we fill a cup with spring water to represent the healing waters of her well that accompanied the Israelites during their 40 years in the desert. This year we will add a Bubbe's Cup filled with fresh-squeezed Florida orange juice as a symbol of the grandmother's return from the promised land of Florida in time to attend the family seder.

Unlike Rashi, we won't delete the song "Had Gadya" because we know too many people who love this nightmare-inducing nursery rhyme about the cat, the dog and the little goat. Likewise, "Echad Mi Yodea" is beloved, no matter how long it takes to sing all the verses.

In fact, this year we will add a few more: "Who knows 14? I know 14. Fourteen are the cold, leftover matzah balls. Who knows 15? I know 15. Fifteen are the trips we make to the kitchen, clearing the table and loading the dishwasher."

We'll end the seder with "Le shanah ha b'ah b'Yerushalayim," the traditional Hebrew phrase that literally means "Next year in Jerusalem." We consider this to be a travel suggestion and would love to do a destination seder next year. While Israel would be great, we've been tempted by glossy advertisements for all-inclusive, weeklong Passover vacations. The kids would surely join us if we celebrate beachside. "Le shanah ha b'ah b'Puerto Rico."

⌒ 11 ⌒

Two Chances to Ring
in the New Year

As Jews, we're lucky to have two chances to celebrate the beginning of a new calendar year. But Rosh Hashanah, the Jewish New Year, is quite different from that other New Year. Let us count down the ways.

10. Resolutions

On the secular New Year's Eve we make resolutions with the best of intentions. We promise to walk on the treadmill for 30 minutes a day, to stop spending $4 on a latte at Starbucks and to give up all refined sugar. At Rosh Hashanah services, we say prayers to begin the 10-day period of repentance because we've long abandoned these resolutions. This repentance comes in handy right after services at the Kiddush when we make a beeline for a nice piece of chocolate *babka* and forget about our diet.

9. Get-togethers

Rosh Hashanah is a family holiday; New Year's Eve is not. On Rosh Hashanah, we entice our kids to come home with brisket and *kugel*; these kids are even tolerant of Cousin Ronnie's embarrassing questions, such as "Do you have a boyfriend yet?" On New Year's Eve, it's embarrassing to admit that you have nowhere to go except to Ronnie's party for the cousins.

8. Same Old, Same Old Tunes

The melody to "Avinu Malkeinu," a Rosh Hashanah prayer, hasn't changed in 5,000 years. Compared with this, "Auld Lang Syne" is a recent hit; it has only been on the charts for 226 years. With both songs the crowd starts off strong, but many trail off after the first line or two and mumble the rest.

7. Cantor vs. DJ

While the cantor is a professional who reads Hebrew and has a beautiful singing voice, the New Year's Eve party disc jockey might be the host's nephew who hooked up his iPhone to a set of speakers. If the DJ doesn't mix it up, he won't get the gig next year, but if the cantor does a Rosh Hashanah remix, the congregation might shout "Dayenu," literally, "enough." No one expects new tunes on Rosh Hashanah; it's surprising enough when the cantor sings the "Hineni" prayer from the back of the room.

6. Musical Instruments

The shofar, the hollowed-out ram's horn that's blown like a trumpet, has a proud tradition: It was sounded on Mount Sinai when the Jewish people received the Ten Commandments. The glitter paper party horn, made in China, comes in an eight-pack for $1.99. When the cantor calls out the notes for the shofar, we happily anticipate the familiar blasts, but when Ryan Seacrest counts down the minutes to midnight, we dread hearing drunk party guests blast their horns.

5. Compulsory Attendance

An old hit song asked "What Are You Doing New Year's Eve?" That's a fair question because staying home alone is not an acceptable answer. What would our friends think if our holiday Facebook post revealed that we sat on our sofa, ate takeout sushi and watched *Sleepless in Seattle* for the eighth time? Actually, they are probably doing the same thing.

No composer ever wrote "What Are You Doing Rosh Hashanah?" because everyone knows the answer is "going to synagogue." Even those with a spotty record of synagogue attendance throughout the year put in an appearance on the High Holidays. That's why we have to park in the overflow lot at the church next door and say "Excuse me" over and over to a full row of people when we sneak out to the bathroom.

4. Staying Awake

The kids make fun of the man who dozes off in synagogue: His eyelids droop, his breathing gets louder, and he doesn't stand up when the ark is opened. We hope the woman sitting next to him gives him the elbow before he starts to snore.

We think it's worse to fall asleep in synagogue than to doze off on New Year's Eve before the clock strikes midnight. When our children were little, we would promise to wake them up for the midnight countdown, but we never did. We know the rule: Don't wake a sleeping child. Now, if our partners start to snore before the ball drops, we just let them be. We don't wake a sleeping husband.

3. Getting All Fapitzed

We know we have to look presentable on Rosh Hashanah. We have memories of our teenage years when September meant getting new back-to-school clothes, and the Jewish holidays were a chance to show them off. We still read *Glamour*, but you won't find us wearing the new fall outfit pictured on page 75. We'll pull out something suitable and reliable from the back of our closet and hope we can still fit into it.

In synagogue, a quick scan of the pews tells us who did buy the latest fall fashions: They are the ones *shvitzing* in their new tweed suits and knee-high leather boots. We aren't enthusiastic about wearing a wool suit when the temperature is still in the 80s.

On New Year's Eve we dig into the closet and pull out the sequined tank top and black crepe pants that we save for fancy occasions. Then we go out into the freezing cold and wish we had worn a wool suit and knee-high leather boots.

2. The Whole Kissing Thing

Any teen can tell you that kissing at midnight on New Year's Eve is a big deal. Teenagers jockey for position so that they are not standing next to the geek from history class when the DJ counts down "10...9...8...."

At Rosh Hashanah services there is no countdown to a big kiss. When the rabbi says, "Let's all turn to page 153," you're not expected to kiss the person sitting next to you.

1. Greetings

The generic "Happy New Year" salutation doesn't differentiate between those who are ringing in the secular New Year and the Jewish New Year. At Rosh Hashanah, those in the know greet a fellow member of the tribe in the supermarket or the carpool line with an enthusiastic "L'shanah tovah." Using the correct Hebrew phrase is shorthand for "I know you are cooking a brisket, and I'll see you in synagogue on Thursday."

So raise your champagne glass and put on your party hat. We're gonna party like it's 5777.

∼ 12 ∼

We Should Atone for This Essay

How could we joke about Yom Kippur, the most solemn day on the Jewish calendar? We shouldn't, but we're going to. Just add it to our tab of things we have to atone for.

Rabbi Joseph Telushkin, who is an expert on these things, said that Yom Kippur is considered a day of sadness because it is a day of fasting. We say: You don't eat. You're hungry. That's sad. And synagogue services that last all day? That's sad, too. Yom Kippur is also usually a grumpy day because you haven't had your morning coffee.

Not everyone fasts all day, but some people pretend to. It's most likely the person who protests too much and announces loudly, "Man, am I hungry from fasting all day!" as he reaches for a bagel and some lox at the break-fast. He probably ate a snack a few hours earlier.

Then there are the people who don't go to services but pretend they did. When the conversation turns to the topic of the rabbi's sermon, the pretenders can simply say, "My rabbi spoke about the situation in Israel." That's a safe bet.

Some of us used to drag our teenagers through a crowd of preschoolers to attend the midafternoon, hour-long family service instead of the five-hour-long regular one. Others go early, right when services start. We get annoyed with the people who wander in three hours late, just as the Torah is being returned to the ark. Never mind that we'll sneak out right after the rabbi's sermon.

If you doze off during Yom Kippur services, the sound of the shofar, a ram's horn blown like a trumpet, will likely wake you up. The renowned Jewish scholar Maimonides wrote that the blasts are meant to wake up the soul. He must have come up with this idea after sitting through a few lengthy services and noticing that people weren't paying attention. But back in 1185, at least the congregants weren't looking down to check their email on their cellphones.

We've been going to synagogue for 50 years. Been there, done that. We know how it ends. The gates are closing, the Book of Life is being written and our fate is being sealed. We're in trouble.

In Hebrew, Yom Kippur literally means "Day of Atonement," and the "Al Het," perhaps the quintessential holiday prayer, recounts a multitude of sins for which the congregation asks forgiveness aloud. These include the sin of speaking ill about others, the sin of dishonesty in business dealings, the sin of immorality, the sin of improper thoughts, and the sin of disrespecting parents and teachers. We are adding a few more to the list:

- The sin of leaving your soda can in the upstairs bathroom wastebasket instead of recycling it.
- The sin of leaving your underwear on the bedroom floor.
- The sin of passing judgment on the woman whose SUV took up two parking spots.
- The sin of telling your husband that the new chair was on sale.
- The sin of leaving such a long phone message that the beep sounds and you have to call back to finish what you were saying.

According to Jewish law, only those who were wronged can grant forgiveness, so it's customary for Jews to ask their friends and family to forgive them for their transgressions during the past year. We know two men who take this very seriously, and every year we forgive them for leaving the toilet seat up and clicking the remote control mercilessly from channel to channel.

When Yom Kippur rolls around again, enjoy the rabbi's sermon and have an easy fast. And if you read about two Philadelphia women who were struck by a bolt of lightning, you'll know who they are.

⌐ 13 ⌐

We Love the
Tchotchkes of Christmas

We're Jewish. Our husbands are Jewish and our kids are Jewish. We've been Jewish for thousands of years. It's not news to us that we don't celebrate Christmas. We've never had a Christmas tree. Never cooked a holiday ham. Never strung the bushes outside our homes with colored lights.

But that doesn't mean we don't enjoy yours.

As our children were growing up, we worked hard to shape their Jewish identity. We drove them to Hebrew school on Sunday mornings, made matzah ball soup for 30 Passover guests, and stayed enthusiastic while packing food baskets with their youth groups. Each December, as their friends were anticipating Christmas, we'd have to remind our children that our family lit Hanukkah candles a week ago, and they had already opened their presents.

Still, we would pile the kids into the car and drive to the Italian neighborhood, where we'd all ooh and aah over the houses with thousands of Christmas lights and the one with the flashing Santa that flew across the roof. If truth be told, we are a bit jealous of your lights. Hanukkah is the Festival of Lights, so why didn't we think of stringing holiday lights along our roof and fence? We have to content ourselves with the glow of nine Hanukkah candles.

Now our kids are grown. Their identities are established. We did our best, and they are making their own choices. We can relax and enjoy the fruitcake and the tinsel.

In the melting pot that is America, we like to see the ingredients. We want to know what you're celebrating. We don't have to share your beliefs to appreciate your holiday and revel in the season. It's out there for everyone to enjoy. In fact, we can't avoid it.

We like getting your Christmas cards. We like seeing the photos of your kids and reading your glowing family updates. "Billy made the travel soccer team again! All the cousins gathered for a fabulous family reunion in Pittsburgh!" We don't own matching Christmas sweaters, but we do admire the fact that you got your husband and your teens to put them on and pose for a photo – and no one was frowning or making bunny ears.

In December, when we go into a department store for a set of sheets or some socks, we're drawn to the aisles crammed with Christmas *tchotchkes*. Tchtochke is the Yiddish word for a cute knickknack or a child's plaything, and we feel like children when we gaze upon the wooden Santas, snow-covered ceramic villages and sparkly mini poinsettia trees.

We wish we had a carton filled with Christmas decorations and ribbon garlands to dress up our living rooms once a year. The lone blue and silver Hanukkah banner we hang in the kitchen just doesn't cut it. We love the tchotchkes of Christmas.

We're honored when you include us in your family's celebration. It makes us feel special, and it gives us an excuse to shop for a Christmas tchtotchke for you. We get a kick out of seeing "our" Santa-on-a-surfboard ornament hanging on your tree.

We enjoy fruitcake with its candied cherries and little bits of citron. We like eggnog, especially with rum. Christmas cookies? Yes, please. We look forward to a friend's annual delivery of homemade, frosted butter cookies shaped like snowmen and angels and reindeer.

People have asked us, "Are you offended if I wish you Merry Christmas?" Of course not. The thought behind your sentiment is sincere. We're comfortable with our minority status, and if you're interested we'd be delighted to tell you all about Hanukkah.

Likewise, we're happy when friends tell us about other traditions: Kwanzaa, the African-American celebration of cultural heritage; Diwali, the Hindu Festival of Lights; and Bodhi Day, the commemoration of Buddha's enlightenment. That's three more sets of holiday decorations for us to enjoy.

One day, we hope to be invited to someone's house to taste the traditional Diwali dessert of gulab jamun, fried dough balls in sugary syrup. They sound similar to sufganiyot, the fried jelly donuts we eat during Hanukkah, and we're sure we'll like them. Invite us and we'll bring you a fringed, orange Diwali lantern to hang in your home.

The Kids Are Home!

⌒ 14 ⌒

Many Happy Returns

Our supermarket bills are doubling, we've done four loads of laundry, and we told the gardener not to blow the leaves at 8 a.m. Our kids have come home from college – home where they're bored, where friends don't live on the same hallway, and where food delivery stops well before midnight.

They'll be home for at least part of the summer, and we're so excited to see them.

When your kids are little, you can't imagine a day when they'll be independent. Then they get on the school bus and disappear. They learn to drive and call you from the city, asking how to get to the big street that leads home. Next thing you know, you're dropping them off at college with clothes, a laptop and a debit card.

We like to pretend that they still need us as much as they used to. And although many things have changed, we have noticed some similarities to the good old days.

When our children were young, they sometimes refused to taste new foods. Now they refuse to eat supermarket sushi. We used to give them $5 a week allowance. Now we slip them cash on the way to the train because we know they need it. They used to love being pushed in the stroller. These days, they borrow our car for "important business." We used to hang every piece of their precious artwork on the refrigerator. Now we "like" their work projects on Facebook.

We still love to spend time with our kids; we fondly remember taking them to the zoo and letting them ride a camel. But those days are long gone, so we do what we can. We dream up family outings that they'll want to be a part of, like a Segway tour or a baseball game. We schedule play dates with their aunts and uncles, who want to see them as much as we do.

When they were little, we would broil a lamb chop just for them. Now when they come home, we cook up a whole rack of lamb. We stock up on their favorite foods, making special trips to the deli for lox and bagels and to the health food store for the orange peach mango juice they like. We're hoping that when they open the refrigerator, they'll be thrilled by how thoughtful their mother is and will want to come home again soon.

We miss our children and their friends. When they're home and we cook dinner, we make extra just in case some of those friends drop by. If the kids decide to go out to eat instead, we don't mind having leftover rib-eye steaks and a big bowl of salad on hand.

The Talmud, the collection of ancient rabbinic laws and commentaries, charges Jewish parents with providing shelter, clothing and food for their children. Strangely enough, it also obliges parents to teach their children to swim – to help make them self-reliant and independent. That was our goal when we taught our kids how to dump in the detergent, twist the dial and throw in a load of laundry. Our kids are self-reliant, but it makes us feel good to do their laundry and fold their rock concert T-shirts.

Our kids feel obliged to bring us up to date on what the young people are doing. They helped an unnamed father make himself a Facebook page and "finally join the modern world." They taught us how to secretly leave one person out of a group message chat without hurting that person's feelings, and they told us that we only have to wear "business-casual" attire from the waist up for a video conference.

Having our children home is wonderful but nerve-wracking because they're used to living by their own rules. At 11:30 p.m. when we're going to bed, they're heading out the front door to "see who's around." While we're gardening and paying bills, they're lounging on the sofa catching up on *Game of Thrones* because they "worked really hard last semester."

We never know how much gas will be left in the car. We stub our toes on sports equipment left in the hall. Our daily routines are disrupted, but we don't mind. A full house fills a mom's heart with joy.

Life is much more exciting when the kids are around.

∽ 15 ∽

Sorting Through a Lifetime of Stuff

Cleaning out our parents' and our in-laws' homes – when they've downsized, moved or died – has made us vow not to put our children through the same task.

Why did they save all this stuff? The breakfront filled with Waterford crystal goblets and two sets of bone china. The shelves lined with Lladro figurines, candlesticks and souvenir plates from their travels. Glossy coffee-table books on baseball and D-Day. Stacks of paperback mysteries. *Golf's Funniest Jokes. Bridge Basics.* A set of encyclopedias from 1964, in case you want to read about the Soviet Union, typewriters and cassette tapes.

In our homes, we already have more than enough stuff. We each have three sets of dishes and flower vases of every size and shape. Our shelves are lined with knick-knacks. We don't have an empty wall on which to hang their art.

We did make room for the photo albums from our childhood, the pretty vegetable dish we always used on Thanksgiving, and the candlesticks from Israel, but we didn't need another dining room table.

When we called in an estate clean-out service, they gave us disappointing news: Our treasures were worth *bubkes*. Very few items had resale value. Would we take a few hundred dollars for the entire lot?

After these sad chores, we were determined to sort through our stuff. We started by offering some of the items to our adult children. We were overjoyed when one child found space in his tiny apartment for the teak kitchen table that had been waiting for him in the attic for 23 years. Another child wanted a bookcase, but not enough of our stuff has found a home with our kids. What can our daughter do with Lenox china for 12 in her rental apartment?

We were sure that none of them would want our old set of encyclopedias from 1990 and that we could safely find the books a new home, but neither the library nor the used bookstore had interest. We were considering cutting them up and using the pictures for craft projects – who were we kidding? – when one son said he might one day want the F book with its flags of countries that no longer exist. The set remains on the shelf.

When we came across a never-opened electronic chess set in the basement that still sported a $99 price tag, we thought it must be valuable. We'd sell it on eBay. Then we found one listed there for $2.50, so we donated ours to Goodwill. The kids have asked us to hold onto their Beanie Babies while they wait for the collectibles market to rebound, so the stuffed animals are still in a giant plastic bag in the basement.

The white painted bureau and matching mirror will be staying in the attic. Down the road it will be perfect for a grandchild. So will the children's books, which we've pared down to one plastic tub of much-loved favorites.

We look forward to the day when our children establish homes of their own with plenty of storage space. We'll pack up and ship their childhood treasures to them.

"Ben, a package came for you today. Did you order Boy Scout badges, old baseball cards, souvenir Playbills and outdated textbooks?"

We have made progress with the clean-out, but there's so much more to do. Each closet and cabinet holds a surprise, such as a Polaroid camera that still works, a junior high school charm bracelet, or 21 silver dollars that were a 21st birthday present. Every item has to be evaluated.

We now understand why our parents kept all their stuff: It's too hard to pare down a lifetime of possessions. Trophies, photos and knickknacks have value only because of the memories attached. That's why our snow globe collection, charity run T-shirts and newspaper clippings – mementos of adventures and accomplishments – haven't been tossed.

We'll admit that we're never going to move into a Tiny House or get joy from living simply with only 100 possessions, especially when our family photo albums, the kids' grade-school ceramic projects, and their hand-drawn Mother's Day cards alone fill up several boxes.

This is valuable stuff, and there still is room in the attic.

～ 16 ～

Our Kids Teach Us
the Darndest Things

When our children were young, we introduced them to the pleasures of childhood – from reading *Goodnight Moon* to riding a two-wheeler. We relished the chance to play with them, teach them and expand their horizons, and we imagined what they would do when they grew up.

We never imagined what they would teach us. Our children have made us more socially conscious, politically correct and tech-savvy. They are patient when they explain to us for the third time how to make a playlist on our cellphone. When they laugh at us because we still have a landline and we pay our bills by snail mail, we know it's because they love us. Our children have taught us well.

Early on, we did the bulk of the teaching: Wash your hands after you use the toilet. Ask permission before you pet the neighbor's dog. Remember to say "please." Long before middle school, they were training us: Don't flush the toilet every time you use it; you're wasting water. Get a dog at a shelter, not a pet store. Never ask a boy if he has a girlfriend because he may be dating a guy. If you have to, you can ask him if he's seeing anyone.

When our daughters were little, we picked out their clothes and dressed them. Now they give us fashion advice. They tell us it's time to give away our "mom jeans," and they teach us eight ways to tie a scarf. Their outlook opens our eyes: Purple hair just means you are creative, not crazy; a tattoo is body art, not a gang symbol; and people get things other than their ears pierced.

We taught them about food: Chicken comes in forms other than nugget. You won't know if you like vegetable curry unless you try it. Who knew that just a few years later they would ask us to try the Lenni-Lenape rabbit stew at their seventh-grade Native American feast?

Our kids informed us that the word for people who don't eat macaroni and cheese is "vegan," not "picky." They taught us that we don't have to eat our green vegetables anymore; we can drink them. Kale comes in a smoothie with beets and wheatgrass; it's served in an eco-friendly glass bottle for $9 at a trendy café. When we crave something sweet at midnight, we don't have to forage for stale Oreos. We can get warm cookies delivered to our door using the "Cookie Craving" app they downloaded for us.

When our children brought home pets and took up hobbies, they got us involved, too: We fed granola to pet rats and frozen mice to a pet snake. We took scuba-diving lessons in a local swimming pool even though we were terrified. We learned how to judge Lincoln-Douglas debates. We now know that "break" and "lock" are useful vocabulary words for both a hip-hop dancer and a wrestler.

When we were growing up, every Jewish kid took piano lessons. Our kids played piano and then some, and we learned that it's easier to deliver a forgotten clarinet than a cello to school. It's harder to find a teacher for the steel drums than the French horn. It's a miracle when the middle-school orchestra ends on the same note at the same time.

Our kids are music *mavens*, and they have over 30,000 songs on their playlists. They've exposed us to musical genres beyond Motown and hard rock. They taught us that grunge doesn't mean it needs to be washed, crunk is not a noise your car makes, and Euro pop is not a German soda.

When we grew up, travel was limited to summers at the beach or winter getaways to Florida. Our kids are world travelers; they've told us that in China you can get a $5 massage from a blind person and that street food is safe to eat if you've watched it being cooked. They also proved to us that it's possible to cram three weeks' worth of clothing in a backpack.

We look forward to the next stage of our kids' lives, by which we mean weddings and babies. None of our kids are there yet. Still, we're eager for them to teach us about digital wedding favors, why it's okay to have a girlfriend be the best man at your wedding, and the proper way to put baby Hudson or Harper to bed in an organic cotton sleep pod.

There's Room in the Tent
for the Whole Mishpuchah

⌒ 17 ⌒

Welcome to the Tribe

A young family just moved into the house on the corner. The name on their mailbox reads "Scott." Are they members of the tribe? What about our new accountant? He did a great job filing our taxes.

While our parents would use the term *landsman* to refer to a fellow Jew, we prefer "member of the tribe" and its abbreviation – MOT. Tribe refers to the biblical 12 tribes of Israel; each was descended from one of Jacob's 12 sons.

We're protective of our tribe's reputation. When people make the headlines for notorious reasons – they robbed a bank, had an affair or cheated on their taxes – we whisper to each other "*Oy*, is he Jewish? What's his last name?" The tribe is close-knit and its numbers are few, so we worry that someone will bring dishonor to the rest of us.

We're grateful to those who bring *kuvid* (honor) to the tribe. We know that Jews are pretty smart, but we were surprised and delighted to learn that 22 percent of all individual recipients of the Nobel Prize since 1901 are MOTs. Some are well known, such as Saul Bellow (Literature) and Albert Einstein (Physics); others are less so. Melvin Schwartz (Physics), your children are very proud of you, and so are we.

Not many Jewish athletes make it to the big leagues, but when they do, we *kvell*. Sandy Koufax, a Cy Young award-winning southpaw pitcher, will always be remembered for refusing to pitch in Game 1 of the 1965 World Series because it fell on Yom Kippur, the holiest day of the Jewish year. Some 31 years earlier, Hank Greenberg, a first basemen for the Detroit Tigers, also refused to play on Yom Kippur in the middle of a pennant race. Greenberg, whose nicknames included "The Hebrew Hammer," was one of the greatest sluggers in baseball history. Way to represent the tribe!

About a dozen baseball players are continuing the proud tradition of Jews in the Major Leagues. Ryan Braun, an outfielder for the Brewers, played in five All-Star Games. Ike Davis once hit three home runs in a single game. We were tickled to read that Ike's given name is Isaac Benjamin; we bet it looked nice engraved on his Bar Mitzvah invitation. We're also embracing all-star African-American basketballer Amar'e Stoudemire. He discovered he had some Jewish roots, made a trip to Israel, and had a Star of David tattooed on his thumb.

Members of the tribe like to guess whether celebrities, politicians and sports figures are also MOTs. One website lets you do just that and then see how others voted: Rock and roller Bruce Springsteen (no); his drummer, Max Weinberg (yes.) Another site renders a verdict on famous people – artists and athletes, scientists and sociopaths, and even fictional characters – from most Jewish (Mel Brooks) to least Jewish (Mel Gibson). Brief bios tell the story: The late Mickey Cohen, a Jewish mob boss who worked with Al Capone, was a member of the tribe. So is Barbie, the plastic Mattel doll. "Don't be misled by the toy's blond hair and blue eyes," the website cautions: Barbie's mother/inventor was Jewish businesswoman Ruth Handler, and Barbie was named for her daughter, Barbara.

In his yearly "Chanukah Song," comedian Adam Sandler sings about "people who are Jewish just like you and me." His list of famous Jews includes Captain Kirk (William Shatner) and Mr. Spock (Leonard Nimoy), The Fonz (Henry Winkler) and Kirk Douglas (born Issur

Danielovitch). We're proud to have Adam Sandler on our list.

The question of "Who is a Jew?" has been debated for thousands of years. Traditionally, a person is Jewish if he or she is born to a Jewish mother or converts to Judaism. More liberal branches of Judaism recognize children born to either a Jewish mother or a Jewish father. They have less stringent laws about conversion, adoption and children who will be raised in Jewish homes. Others say that to include yourself in the tribe, it's enough to self-identify as Jewish, keep a Jewish home and raise your children with Jewish traditions.

We welcome them all. We're such a small tribe that we're always looking for new members, particularly those who make us proud. There's plenty of room in the tent.

∽ 18 ∽

Mama Loshen by the Ocean

There's something about Jews and the beach. We love the ocean and the salty sea air. It's in our genes.

Our great-grandparents relaxed by the shores of the Black Sea. Our grandparents would go to Brighton Beach to escape the stifling heat of the Lower East Side. Our parents would pack us into the back of the station wagon with suitcases and bags of groceries and off we'd go to the Jersey Shore. It was close by, easy and inexpensive compared with other vacation spots. And the beach was free and open to everyone to enjoy.

We are not so fond of lakes. In fact, you're unlikely to find Jews at a lake unless it's in our lukewarm memories of Jewish summer camp and its cold murky lake with a disgusting muddy bottom, scummy edges, and all those creepy nameless fish that could swim up and bite us at any time.

In the first half of the 20th century, working-class Jews from Philadelphia flocked to Atlantic City. Women strolled the Boardwalk in mink coats and high heels – occasionally getting a heel stuck between the boards on their way to see Benny Goodman play at Steel Pier. The whole *mishpuchah* (family) rented rooms in a guesthouse for a week or two; cousins fished off the jetties and played gin rummy at night.

New York Jews made family memories at Brighton Beach, where they might have encountered Irving Berlin, who worked as a singing waiter there. When they had enough swimming, they'd take the kids to nearby Coney Island for Nathan's Famous hot dogs and amusement rides.

As Jews found prosperity, they ventured to more upscale beach towns. Philadelphians went to Margate and Ventnor; New Yorkers frequented Rockaway and later the Hamptons.

Today you'll find Jewish enclaves anywhere there are sandy beaches and saltwater tides, and if you hang out at a beach where the tribe gathers, you may hear some of these Yiddish words floating on the cool ocean breeze:

Shlep: Anyone with little kids knows the joys of *shlepping* plastic buckets and shovels, boogie boards, chairs, umbrellas and coolers filled with drinks and snacks to the beach – and then having to shlep it all home. We miss making sand castles and lifting the kids over the incoming waves, but we don't miss lugging their stuff. We're grateful that they're now big enough to shlep their own chairs and beach bags.

Nosherei: We could walk back to the house for a tuna fish sandwich, but it's more fun to walk up and down the Boardwalk snacking on fudge, salt water taffies, french fries, pizza and soft ice cream. All these foods qualify as *nosherei*.

Ongepotchket: When we go to the beach, we're all *ongepotchket*, thrown together. We wear big hats to shield our faces from sunburn, comfortable T-shirts to cover up what the slimming swimsuit can't, and cheap rubber flip-flops for padding down the walkway. We are not all *fapitzed* like the women who wear diamond tennis bracelets, gold earrings and makeup to the beach. Their bathing suit cover-ups are dressier than what we wear to dinner. You can guess which women go into the ocean.

Shpilkes: Kids who have been cramped up in Bubbe and Zayde's tiny beach house all week without access to their favorite toys and TV shows can get *shpilkes*, or ants in their pants. To help them blow off some of their nervous energy, we give them $10 for the arcade. When we get shpilkes from all this vacation togetherness, we retreat to a quiet corner of the backyard and dive into Amazon's "best summer beach read."

Chazerai: When the kids come home from the arcade and show us the two plastic snakes, eight jeweled rings, three mini-superballs and the Chinese finger trap they picked out so painstakingly, we say, "Take all that *chazerai* off the kitchen table."

Shluff: After the kids spend a day splashing in the ocean, riding the waves, chasing the ice cream man, burying siblings up to their necks in the sand, playing in the outdoor shower, running down the Boardwalk, riding the Tilt-A-Whirl and begging for cotton candy, we can only hope that they *gai shluffy* (go to sleep) early so that we can mix up some margaritas and relax.

～ 19 ～

A Balabusta in Buckingham Palace?

When Kate Middleton was preparing to marry Prince William, we received an email implying that the future queen had Jewish roots. This whole scenario was dreamed up because Kate's maternal grandparents, Ronald Goldsmith and Dorothy Harrison, have Jewish-sounding surnames. We know better than to make assumptions like this; after all, Beatle George Harrison was Catholic before he embraced Hinduism. We also read that generations of Kate's family have been baptized in churches and married in cathedrals.

This didn't stop us from imagining what the Duchess of Cambridge would do if she were to embrace her doubtful Jewish heritage and become a *balabusta*.

After the wedding, Kate's first order of business would be to hang a mezuzah, a parchment scroll with a verse from the Torah, on each of Kensington Palace's many doors – the front door, the west door, the gallery door, the drawing room door and the 53 other doors. We're sure there's a footman with a hammer and nails who can help her.

If the young couple want to keep kosher, it won't be a problem to have two sets of dishes. Will and Kate could make the Royal Worcester Evesham china *milchig* (dairy) for serving blintzes or cheese sandwiches and the Wedgwood Boleyn set *fleishig* (meat) for pheasant under glass.

Observing Shabbat, the Jewish Sabbath, shouldn't be difficult either because we're certain that there are many sets of ornate silver candlesticks in the castle cupboards. Kate will have to tell the chamberlain to tell the butler to tell the cook that she'll need a large challah for Friday night dinner. And for the menu? Skip the pheasant under glass. Roast a nice chicken instead.

William can keep his beloved fish and chips. Perfectly kosher. Pickled onions, another traditional British pub favorite, are also acceptable. Should the prince get the urge for a little haggis, Kate could say, "Honey, we call it *kishka* now."

Passover will present a challenge. Just imagine how long will it take to clean out the crumbs from the butler's pantry, the master cook's prep room, the scullery and the palace kitchen, which has enough ovens to cook brisket for 200 guests. Kate will have to get rid of the Scottish shortbread and stock up on cans of macaroons.

Remember those crazy hats that got so much attention at the royal wedding? Instead of saving her fascinators for the Royal Ascot races and the Order of the Garter procession, Kate can trot hers out for Rosh Hashanah and Yom Kippur services. She'll fit right in, sitting in the front row of the synagogue.

Of course, Will and Kate will be invited to the next Jewish Federation Young Leadership cocktail party, but will the Prince be part of the Real Estate Division or the Future Kings Division? Kate better remind him to bring his business cards to exchange with the other up-and-coming big *machers*.

When Kate joins her girlfriends for Girls Night Out, they can get mani-pedis or take in a movie. After her book club finishes *The Princess Diaries*, Kate can suggest that they tackle *The Red Tent*.

Fast forward a few years: The arrival of the royal babies stirred up our imaginations again. Great Grand-mom Queen Bubbe Elizabeth is surely *kvelling* over Prince George, the future king of England, and his sister, Princess Charlotte Elizabeth Diana. When the great grandchildren come to visit, she'll instruct the servants to put away her precious *tchotchkes* and bring out the Beatrix Potter collection of Beanie Babies.

How cute Georgie will look in a *yarmulke* embroidered with a little gold crown and his big title – His Royal Highness Prince George of Cambridge! How easy it will be for Princess Charlotte to find a crown when she wants to play dress up and be Queen Esther!

We're so excited to watch them grow up, but we won't be holding our breath waiting to be invited to their B'nai Mitzvah record hops at Buckingham Palace. However, we've heard that the royal seder table seats 67. Perhaps there will be room for us.

Excuse Us While We Kvetch

〜 20 〜

Too Many Mavens

When we say "*maven*," we conjure up an image of an expert who's Jewish, like our stockbroker, who recommended we buy Apple in 2006, or our friend Judi, who knows how to get early access to the Nordstrom Anniversary Sale. We also use the word to refer to someone – Jewish or not – who is knowledgeable about a Jewish subject: "He knows everything about smoked fish. He's a lox maven." "He's gone on three digs in Israel. He's a maven of biblical archeology."

Then there are double mavens: Jews who are an authority on a Jewish subject. Cookbook author Joan Nathan is a double maven of the Jewish kitchen. She knows everything about Jewish food, from Sephardic *kugels* to New York *knishes*. Leo Rosten, author of *The Joys of Yiddish*, is a double maven of Yiddish words. He's the expert at distinguishing a *k'nocker* (a showoff) from a *macher* (a big wheel).

We consider ourselves to be double mavens, too. We are Jewish *and* we love Jewish words. We even wrote a Jewish dictionary in which we defined hundreds of words including *chutzpah*. And then we realized that we have chutzpah proclaiming ourselves The Word Mavens!

These days, it seems like everyone's a maven.

Mississippi cookbook author Martha Hall Foose is lauded as a "cookbook maven." If she's really a maven, shouldn't she have recipes for knishes and *rugelach* – along with deviled eggs and skillet-fried corn – in her collection?

June Ambrose is a celebrity stylist who has worked with Mary J. Blige and Mariah Carey. She's been called a "style maven." Since she's a maven, she should know what to do when Mariah demands, "No more *shmattes*. I want to be all *fapitzed* for the Grammys."

Martha Stewart is a multi-maven. She's been labeled a "media maven," "homemaking maven," "food maven" and "entertaining maven," but she's the only maven we know who reaches for the ornaments, twinkle lights and pine boughs to decorate her holiday table. We think Martha is more of a *macher* than a maven.

Real gurus suffer a similar fate: They have to compete with loads of self-proclaimed gurus who have no relation to a real Hindu spiritual teacher. (We suspect that real gurus are less *kvetchy* about pretenders than we are.)

Beauty gurus know all about blush, not bindis. Tech gurus can bring your computer back to life but cannot reincarnate your old one into a MacBook Air. Travel gurus promise to find you cheap airfare and the best all-inclusives, but can they get you a deal at a silent meditation retreat in an ashram in India? A true guru can.

One online job site boasts that it has a global pool of "over 400,000 gurus eager to help with your technical and business needs." Do they guarantee that you'll remain spiritually centered when your Excel spreadsheet refuses to load?

Guru and maven are not the only self-proclaimed titles; many people lay claim to royalty. Californian Todd Spanier, the King of Mushrooms, traces his royal mushroom lineage to his grandparents, who taught him how to forage for fungi when he was a youngster. Freddy Zeideia is the King of Falafel. He holds the title of New York's #1 Street Vendor. He's expanded his kingdom to include a truck, a cart and a restaurant. Pat Olivieri is the King of Steaks. His family's Philadelphia cheesesteak business has occupied this throne since 1930.

Fewer people claim the title of Prince. Thank goodness the real ones – England's Prince William and Prince Harry – come up high on a Google search. Imagine how they would feel if the Prince of Gardening and the Prince of Sandwiches were ranked above them. Note: The Earl of Sandwich is actual royalty; the Duke of Earl is not.

With so many titles up for grabs, we asked ourselves, "Do we want to stick with Word Mavens or try something else?" Word Princesses is awkward and evokes Disney characters who can't spell. Word Queens sounds like we should be on a reality TV show, designing evening gowns out of dictionary pages. Should we consider Word Gurus? It does have a certain spiritual cachet.

So we made a comparison: A maven is loud and boisterous and shouts hello; a guru whispers and prays that you find inner peace. A maven gets all fapitzed; a guru sports a simple cotton robe. A maven is always up for a *nosh* and will bring the *babka*. A guru comes empty-handed because he's on a sacred fast.

We'll stick with maven.

∽ 21 ∽

The Trouble With Digital Nudniks

We're as accustomed to technology as any middle-aged women can be. We friend, text, blog and Snapchat. But lately, AutoCorrect has been getting on our nerves. We're tired of being continually corrected by him and his older brother, Spell Check, when they don't know what to do with our Yiddish words.

When we neglected to capitalize the "J" in Jewish, AutoCorrect changed "jewish" to "jewfish." When we started to type the word *"fapitzed"* (all dolled up), Auto-Correct switched it to "baptized." These words have some letters in common but not much else – although have you seen some of those babies who get all fapitzed in lace-trimmed, organza baptism gowns?

Without asking permission, AutoCorrect jumps right in with what he thinks is best. How dare he suggest we mean "nude" instead of *"nudnik"*? We know a nudnik – a nuisance – when we meet one, and AutoCorrect is a nudnik!

Spell Check has better manners than his brother. He gently expresses his concern with a wiggly red underline, offers a few suggestions, and then steps aside if we click to ignore him.

While Spell Check knows how to spell words, he doesn't always know how to use them. We've been telling our kids for years that he won't warn them that it's wrong to "put there book over their." Homonyms always make Spell Check *farblondjet*, confused.

Why are these digital nudniks such know-it-alls? They apparently studied with Vladimir Levenshtein, the Russian scientist who devised a way to measure the distance between two words. With one keystroke, a Levenshtein distance of 1, "stack" becomes "snack"; with two keystrokes, "dove" becomes "dive" and then "dine." Levenshtein's algorithm is the basis of Spell Check, AutoCorrect and other smart-aleck computer programs.

Levenshtein distance brings to mind the Six Degrees of Kevin Bacon. We don't know who Vladimir Levenshtein is, but if we apply his theory, didn't he once date our old friend Sue Goldstein's sister's college roommate who knew Lenny Shusterman? Jews don't need to figure out their six degrees of separation because we're all *mispuchah*, family.

We have to admit that in some ways AutoCorrect reminds us of ourselves. Like us, he can be helpful, funny, right (sometimes) and annoying (now and again). Even though we complain about him, the truth is that we're jealous of his ability to pop up at any time with an unsolicited suggestion. That's every mother's dream. Imagine if we could pop in long distance when our kids were on a first date and give a thumb's up or thumb's down on the match.

We're willing to coexist with our irritating digital proofreaders. We've discovered the tab that let's us dismiss Spell Check by clicking "Ignore All." We'll make peace with AutoCorrect – as long as he leaves our names alone. It's Scolnic, not Scenic. And Eisenberg does not follow that "*i* before *e* except after *c*" rule.

22

Four Questions, Three Matzot and Too Many Choices

When we were kids, we had fewer choices. Watching TV meant three channels, not 300. A cup of coffee was instant or perked, not pressed or siphoned. Buying sneakers meant deciding on Converse or Keds, and jeans had bell-bottoms or straight legs.

Passover, the weeklong holiday that celebrates the Israelites' freedom from slavery in Egypt, was simpler then, too. We had just one recipe for haroset, the mixture that symbolized the mortar the Israelites used to make bricks for the pyramids. It had apples and walnuts – not dates, pistachios and ginger. There was just one decorative goblet on the table for the prophet Elijah. Moses' sister, Miriam, was left out. Hosts bought a big bottle of Manischewitz Concord Grape wine and didn't worry if it paired well with roast chicken or salty fish appetizers. There was no need to buy a kosher-for-Passover Israeli Chardonnay.

Today Manischewitz sells six kinds of matzah ball mix and 16 varieties of Tam Tam crackers. In all, more than 300 new items hit the Passover shelves last year.

We understand why Russian immigrants, for whom shopping used to mean standing in a breadline, were bewildered when they entered an American supermarket for the first time and encountered the abundance and variety of consumer goods.

That's how we feel when it comes time for Passover shopping.

Remember when macaroons, the chewy, flourless, ball-shaped cookies made with shredded coconut and egg whites, came in vanilla, chocolate and chocolate chip only? Now manufacturers introduce new flavors each year, and the supermarket display is stocked with Red Velvet, Carrot Cake, Double Chocolate Gluten-Free and Rocky Road. Ooh! Rocky Road. We eagerly broke the seal and dove into the can, only to discover that it was the same old chocolate chip macaroon with a small shred of marshmallow added in. We were disappointed.

Don't confuse Passover macaroons with French macarons, the brightly colored, meringue-and-almond sandwich cookies that cruise around the city on food trucks. Though their spellings are close, they are not at all alike. Macarons don't yet come kosher for Passover, so we'll wait rather than make them ourselves. While we can deftly form a clumpy coconut ball, we're sure to squish a delicate meringue disc.

These days, shopping requires soul-searching. Should we buy chicken broth labeled "organic and low-sodium," "free range and low-fat" or "100% natural and no MSG"? We find a box that promises all of the above, but it costs twice as much. We also have to debate the merits of tried and true versus something new. That turns out to be easy. The new "light, whole-wheat bran matzah" doesn't even tempt us. We'll stick with the same old same old.

When it comes to *gefilte fish*, there are fewer choices. Gefilte fish don't swim in any ocean; their native habitat is the supermarket. They are neither farm-raised nor wild; they are tame and bland and held captive in a glass jar filled with gelatinous goo.

This Passover we were drawn to the Rokeach brand because we saw the Yiddish word *haimish* on the label – haimish as in unpretentious, homey and informal. We would enjoy an appetizer that fits this description, but how exactly can gefilte fish be unpretentious? Do they just sit there politely and wait to be eaten?

While we don't know any haimish fish, we do know some pretentious gefilte fish. We're referring to the sustainably sourced, artisanal, small-batch loaves with a layer of salmon on top that are made by hipster chefs. Our mass-produced gefilte fish have no illusions that they are special. They know they are no better than their jar mates.

When Passover approaches each year, we go online, find new holiday recipes and bookmark those that look good. As Ashkenazic Jews who grew up eating Eastern European fare, we are intrigued by the Sephardic Passover recipes: stuffed grape leaves (Greece), basmati rice with stewed fruits (Morocco), and chickpea dumplings (Iran), among others.

Until this year, we could look but not touch. That's because Ashkenazic Jews have had to avoid kitniyot (rice, beans, corn, peanuts, lentils and seeds) since the 13th century. The worry was that some hametz, the leavened grain products prohibited to all Jews during Passover, might get mixed into the burlap sack along with their two rubles of rice.

In December 2015, the Rabbinical Assembly, the governing body of the Conservative movement of Judaism, declared kitniyot kosher for Passover. Now it's on the up and up to put peanut butter on our matzah, serve rice pilaf with our roast chicken, and snack on hummus and popcorn during Passover. This all sounds good to us, but we won't be serving chickpea dumplings in place of matzah balls in our chicken soup. That would never fly.

We appreciate having lots of choices, but we get tired of making them. So at Passover we'll make it easy for ourselves. We'll pass over the "new and improved" super-tasty matzah, the "bigger and better" *pesachdik* granola bars, and the "self-cooking" chicken in a bag. We'll stick with tradition.

⌢ 23 ⌣

Confidence or Cockiness?
Just Call It Chutzpah

Your friend asks you to throw her daughter a baby shower. Then she emails you a list of 50 guests and suggests a champagne brunch at a nice restaurant.

It's rumored that your company is going under, and the president has called a news conference. You've had a great sales year, so you march right in and ask for the raise you feel you deserve.

Your neighbor borrows your lawn mower and keeps it for three weeks. When you walk next door to get it back, your neighbor informs you that your mower is no good, and it's time for you to replace it.

Confidence or cockiness? You decide, but no matter where you draw the line, there is no question that all of the above are examples of *chutzpah*, defined by the *Merriam-Webster* dictionary as "personal confidence or courage that allows someone to do or say things that may seem shocking to others." Synonyms for chutzpah, which comes from the Hebrew word khuspa, include audacity, brazenness, cheekiness, insolence, impudence, gall – and balls.

The first known use of the word was in 1883. That was also the year of the first telephone call between New York City and Chicago. Coincidence? We think not.

Ring, ring.

"No we don't want a subscription to *The New York Times.* You have some chutzpah calling and interrupting our dinner!"

Some people attribute chutzpah to an abundance of ego. What else could explain a candidate who spends millions of dollars and months of his life campaigning for president when he only gets 6 percent of the primary vote, or a rock star who demands animal-print throw rugs, a smoothie station and rose petals in her dressing room?

In a comedy skit called "Chutzpah," funny ladies Carol Burnett and Lucille Ball played savvy cleaning ladies who worked at a talent agency. "Here I am, get out of my way, I'm coming on strong. I've got chutzpah," they sang. They called chutzpah "a quality that could propel you to the top."

Maybe this is what the first-ever Jewish hip-hop supergroup, featuring Dr. Dreck and MC Meshugenah, was counting on when it named itself Chutzpah. Just starting out in the music biz and calling yourself a supergroup? Now that's chutzpah!

More than a century after its first known use, chutzpah is still alive and kicking. When we searched online for chutzpah, an ad popped up: "Looking for more chutzpah products?" Did they mean chutzpah deodorant? It doesn't work and you smell terrible, but no one has the nerve to tell you. Chutzpah boots? They'll stomp on anything that gets in their way.

Indeed, the internet is a hotbed of chutzpah: miracle diets, medical treatments with no side effects, and "the perfect love match for you found in less than five minutes."

Chutzpah is such a descriptive word that people of all ethnicities are co-opting it. An Indian newspaper wrote about "Delhi's new diplomatic chutzpah." Another paper called out China for having the chutzpah to "condone hacking and industrial espionage." We consider it Indian chutzpah when the guy behind us in line at Tandoori Kitchen pushes ahead and shouts, "I just want an order for takeout!" And Chinese chutzpah? We'll never forget the cookie with this fortune: "Confucius says be generous when leaving a tip."

People regard examples of chutzpah with grudging admiration or disgust. Writer James Harbeck is on the admiration side. He wrote, "Chutzpah has more guts than nerve does, even more than balls does. And neither nerve nor balls conveys the kind of intelligence that chutzpah conveys."

Yiddish scholar Michael Wex is among the naysayers; he believes that there is nothing good about chutzpah. "It's an unambiguously negative quality characterized by a disregard for manners, social conventions and the feelings and opinions of others," he wrote in *Tablet* magazine. "Chutzpah includes a sense of entitlement. Chutzpah goes to its best friend's funeral and then propositions the bereaved spouse during the shivah [the period of mourning] because there was no chance to do so at the graveside."

Judges don't seem to be fond of chutzpah either. Chutzpah first made its way to the Supreme Court in 1998, when Italian Catholic Justice Antonin Scalia used the word to describe the National Endowment for the Arts' brazenness in asking for government funding. Since then, the word has appeared in hundreds of court decisions. Judges have noted defendants' "staggering chutzpah," "mega chutzpah," "unbridled chutzpah" and "mutual chutzpah" – in a case where each party asked that its court costs be paid by the other side.

We offer up this example of mind-boggling chutzpah. An editor at *Cooks Source* magazine allegedly reprinted an article from the internet without the author's permission. When the author found out and asked for an apology, she was told that she should be happy the magazine didn't put someone else's name on her article or bill her for editing it. As fellow writers, we have *rachmones* (empathy) for the author.

Some people think that chutzpah is the key to the survival of the Jewish people. In fact, that's what Alan Dershowitz, attorney and outspoken defender of Israel, asserted in his 1991 book, *Chutzpah*. Dershowitz himself showed a lot of chutzpah when defending celebrity clients like Mike Tyson, Patty Hearst and O.J. Simpson. He's also one smart cookie: At age 28 he became the youngest full professor of law in Harvard Law School's history.

Moses and Abraham were also clever guys who had more than their fair share of chutzpah. Moses bickered with God when God ordered him back to the land of Egypt. Abraham took the side of the sinners, arguing with God over the destruction of Sodom and Gomorrah. It took a lot of chutzpah to question the all-knowing, all-seeing God. And you think it takes a lot of chutzpah to speak up to your boss!

Shalom means both hello and goodbye, and when someone greets you with this Hebrew word, you'll know the meaning by whether they're coming or going. Chutzpah also has two meanings. If a friend says, "You've got chutzpah!" you could fret over whether she means you're confident or cocky or if she thinks your behavior was admirable or abominable.

Or you could display some chutzpah and just say, "Thanks for the compliment."

Food
Fights

~ 24 ~

Rugelach v. Shnecken: The Jury's Still Out

When we asked *bubbes* who love to bake and friends who love to *nosh* to give us the lowdown on *rugelach* and *shnecken*, they told us, "You should taste my sister's cinnamon rugelach!" or "My husband hates it when I put nuts in the shnecken." They couldn't tell us what differentiated these two bite-sized pastries.

Jewish delis weren't any more helpful. Some label these pastries shnecken; others call them rugelach.

So it was *bashert* (fated) that we came across a van covered with photographs of shnecken. We knew it was shnecken – not rugelach – because "The Schnecken Lady" was emblazoned above the pictures.

We called The Schnecken Lady, Myrna Freedman, hoping she could referee the controversy. (We have manners, so we didn't open the conversation by telling her that she spells it wrong. She doesn't need that first "c" in schnecken.) Myrna told us that she's been baking shnecken since 1977. She uses her Aunt Minnie's recipe; it includes cinnamon sugar, walnuts, raisins and orange marmalade, which gives the pastry its characteristic stickiness.

Myrna declined to take sides. "Call it what you want. The ingredients are basically the same. It depends on how you cut them, what your family calls them, and where you live. In New York, everything's a rugelach."

Thanks, Myrna, but you've clearly taken sides. "Schnecken" is printed on your van, business cards, website and bakery boxes.

We needed to do more research; after all, someone had to take on this delicious investigation. We did our due diligence by examining – and by this we mean eating – as many rugelach and shnecken as humanly possible, and this is what we learned:

The dough: Shnecken dough is typically composed of butter, flour, egg yolks and yeast. It's the same yeasty dough that bakers would use to make coffee cakes, sticky buns and *lekakh*, honey cake.

In Eastern Europe, rugelach was made from the same dough. When these pastries came to America, someone had the bright idea to remove the yeast and add cream cheese. Rugelach came to be known as "cream cheese cookies."

At Lipkin's, a kosher bakery in Northeast Philadelphia that's been in business for four generations, the lady behind the bakery counter told us, "Of course Mitch [Lipkin] puts cream cheese in the dough." Lipkin's sells chocolate, raspberry and cinnamon sugar varieties and calls them rugelach. "I've never heard the word shnecken," the clerk said.

The shape: *New York Times* food critic Mimi Sheraton called shnecken "cinnamon-nut snails" in her book, *From My Mother's Kitchen.* That's an apt description because the word shnecken means snail in German. To get the snail shape, you roll out the dough into a rectangle, spread the filling on top, roll it up like a jelly roll, cut it into small slices, and bake. In Germany and the Austro-Hungarian Empire, the pastries were often eaten at breakfast.

What's the shape of a rugelach? Cookbook author Joan Nathan explained, "'Rug' means spiral or crescent-shaped in Russian, Ukrainian and Polish. A miniature spiral-shaped dough was, therefore, called a rugelach." To get the spiral shape, you roll out the dough into a circle, spread the filling on top, cut it into pie-shaped wedges and, beginning at the wide edge, roll it up to the point like a crescent roll.

The filling: The basic filling for both pastries is a combination of sugar, cinnamon and nuts. Raisins are the next most popular addition. Then there's chocolate, apricot jam and even Nutella.

In recent years, chefs have introduced savory versions of these pastries. One Philadelphia restaurant fills the dough with chicken and *shmaltz* or with salmon, boursin and kimmel seeds. "Have some rugelach," the Israeli-born manager announced as he brought them to our table in place of bread. We asked him why he didn't call them shnecken; he told us he had never heard that word. They were delicious.

Although our research methods may be suspect (pastry bribes were accepted), we did reach a conclusion: It seems that what you call this nosh depends on your family background – not on the dough, shape or filling. Unless you are a direct descendant of German, Austrian or Hungarian Jews, you probably didn't grow up with shnecken. The vast majority of American Jews – and deli owners – are children of immigrants from Poland, Russia and the Ukraine, countries where rugelach ruled, which means that you're more likely to see these pastries labeled rugelach rather than shnecken.

For a last word on the rugelach v. shnecken debate, we turned again to Joan Nathan. She's written about cream cheese and yeast, spirals and snails, and how the best shnecken are sticky like a cinnamon bun. Her conclusion? "Sometimes the pastries seem to be different only in name. If nothing else, the different names offer the perfect excuse to start the day with a shnecken and end it with a rugelach."

That sounds great, Joan. If you ever come over for coffee, we'll be sure to have both on hand.

～ 25 ～

You Say Wonton;
We Say Kreplach

"**P**umpernickel is Jewish; white bread is *goyish*," said comedian Lenny Bruce in the early 1960s, asserting that Jews instinctively categorize everything as Jewish or not.

We're guilty, especially when it comes to food: We say that mayonnaise is goyish and mustard is Jewish. Vichyssoise, the cold potato soup, is goyish; *borscht*, the cold beet soup, is Jewish. An egg is just an egg until you cook it: Then, deviled eggs are goyish; egg salad is Jewish.

Much has changed on the culinary landscape since Lenny Bruce got arrested for saying "*shmuck*" onstage. These days, we are just as likely to eat chicken tikka masala as a corned beef sandwich and to order salmon atop sushi rice instead of a bagel, but we are especially fond of foods that evoke our *bubbes'* kitchens, foods that are honorary members of the tribe. This may explain why the two of us eat chopped liver but not liver pâté.

Knishes make an appearance at many a Yom Kippur break-fast and Bar Mitzvah cocktail hour, but they weren't always saved for special occasions. At the turn of the last century, Jewish immigrants brought knishes to work in their lunchboxes, just like Irish workers packed meat pies. Although both taste best still warm from the oven, they were designed to be portable and could be eaten cold.

In fact, almost every country has a doughy pastry filled with potatoes, vegetables or meat. The Spanish empanada, the Indian samosa and the Italian calzone are all cousins to the knish. Given a choice, we order "One kasha knish and one mushroom knish, please."

We're not as fond of borscht. We remember when cold beet soup would make an appearance on our childhood dinner tables. The grown-ups would swirl a dollop of sour cream into the magenta-colored liquid, and we would cringe in horror and hope they didn't ask us to taste it.

Borscht was a staple in Eastern Europe because beets were plentiful. (So were potatoes, and we much prefer the *latkes* and *kugels* they turned into.) Leafy greens were scarce with the exception of sorrel, which explains why borscht has a cold green cousin named *shav* that's made from sorrel's sour leaves. These days, cooks combine spinach with sorrel to mellow out the shav, but we don't know anyone who actually eats it.

Thanks to farmers markets and the bounty of our gardens, we have no shortage of vegetables. In summer, it's hard to find a restaurant that doesn't have gazpacho on its menu. We often order it. For us, tomatoes, cucumbers and red peppers in a cold soup trump beets any day.

Gefilte fish has a fancy French cousin – the quenelle. Both are made with chopped fish, but then they swim in opposite directions. Quenelles are held together with breadcrumbs; gefilte fish is bound with matzah meal. Quenelles are served hot in a creamy béchamel sauce; gefilte fish is dumped cold from the jar onto a lettuce leaf and dressed up with a carrot curl. We found a recipe for quenelles in *Larousse Gastronomique*, a bible of French cuisine; our recipe for gefilte fish is scrawled on a stained index card that Aunt Miriam pressed into our hand at Passover in April 1986.

While both lox and gravlax come from salmon, we'd never ask the deli guy for a half-pound of gravlax. We call it lox, which is the Yiddish word for salmon. While both are cured in salt, gravlax is also cured in sugar, dill and other spices. You can distinguish the two by the company they keep. Lox is served on a bagel *shmeered* with cream cheese. If you want to be fancy, you can add a little red onion and a slice of cucumber. Gravlax keeps company with brown bread triangles, capers and lemon slices.

Texas barbecue is described as meat cooked "low and slow," which sounds just like the way we cook our brisket. Both start out from the same cut of beef. If you rub the meat with spices and smoke it over mesquite, it becomes a cowboy brisket sandwich, served on a paper plate alongside beans. If you roast it on a bed of onions and carrots, put some tomato sauce on top, cover the pan with aluminum foil, and put it in the oven for hours, it becomes a Jewish holiday favorite that's served on a china dinner plate beside kugel. Much like the Friday night roast chicken, there's nothing uniquely Jewish about brisket – except that we say so.

And one more thing: You know those long, crunchy cookies they sell at Starbucks – the ones with the label that says "biscotti"? Well, they're not. We say they're *mandelbrodt*.

～ 26 ～

Kibitzing About Kugel

When you want another piece of that delicious noodle pudding, do you ask for *kugel* (COO-gul) or *kigel* (KEE-gul)? How you pronounce it is a clue to where your ancestors came from. Galitzianers called it kigel and preferred it sweet. They came from southeastern Poland and the western Ukraine, which included the cities of Chelm and Krakow. Litvaks called it kugel and preferred it savory. They came from Lithuania, northern Poland and northern Russia, which included Vilna, Minsk and Kiev.

Historically, these two groups of Ashkenazic Jews feuded over which one was smarter and higher class, but these distinctions are long gone. Today Jewish battle lines are more likely drawn over which sleepaway camp your kids attend or which Chinese restaurant you call for Sunday night takeout.

But in South Africa, calling out "kugel" can still cause you trouble. That's because it's a derogatory term for a Jewish woman who is materialistic and pretentious.

Why label someone a kugel? Because a kugel is a plain pudding that masquerades as a delicacy. Maybe this explains why when you search online for kugel, among all the photos of noodles, apples and cinnamon deliciousness you come across a photo of a sexy woman with the unfortunate name of Olivia Kugel.

Before a kugel was a kugel, it was a dumpling that was formed from a batter of bread and eggs and simmered in stew; later on, chefs would cook the dumpling in a kugeltopf. (In German kugel means ball; topf is a round earthenware jar.) On Friday afternoons, a Jewish woman would tuck her kugeltopf into her pot of *cholent*, a stew of meat, beans and potatoes, and *shlep* it to the village bakery so it could be placed in a bread oven that was still warm from baking loaves of challah. When the woman picked up her stew at the end of Shabbat, the steamy oven would have turned the dumpling into a pudding.

As time went on, cooks substituted noodles for the bread batter. Traditional Shabbat kugels were served as a side dish to a meat entrée and had to be dairy free to conform to kashrut, the Jewish dietary laws. These savory kugels were usually bound together with eggs and oil; onions sautéed in *shmaltz* were added for flavor. Polish cooks get credit for "inventing" sweet dairy kugels by adding raisins, cinnamon and farmer's cheese; these were a perfect accompaniment for a dairy brunch or lunch. The Ottomans brought rice kugels to Eastern Europe. And in the *shtetl*, where potatoes were eaten several times a day, potato kugel was a treat.

Kugel came to America with Eastern European Jews. In 1871, *Mrs. Esther Levy's Jewish Cookery Book*, the first Jewish cookbook published in America, included a recipe for kugel. Her version was sweet, with raisins, sugar, eggs and homemade noodles.

Some 80 years earlier, when Hasidic Jews began moving from Eastern Europe to Jerusalem, they took their unique sweet and savory kugel recipe with them: It called for very thin noodles combined with eggs, caramelized sugar and lots of freshly ground pepper. The kugel, which was baked in a loaf or tube pan and cut like a cake, became known as Kugel Yerushalmi, or Jerusalem Kugel.

In the last 150 years, kugels have traveled from Vilna to the East Village. Designer three-layer kugels include sweet potatoes, broccoli and cauliflower, or goat cheese, duck eggs and sour cherries. Instead of challah crumbs, chefs spread kosher Japanese panko on top. Kugels have broken out of square and rectangular molds; they are being baked in cookie cutters and in tiny Bundt pans.

If we served a sour cherry kugel baked in a tiny Bundt pan, there would be an uprising. Every family has its favorite kugel variation – and that's the best one. One camp likes its kugel savory with the thinnest of noodles, cottage cheese, cream cheese and a little vanilla. No fruit, no pineapple chunks, no strange foreign objects. Another contingent likes its kugel sweet with brown sugar, raisins and extra wide egg noodles.

No matter what they look like, kugels are one of the most ubiquitous Jewish comfort foods. They are on the table at holiday dinners and charity luncheons. We know people who wrap kugel in aluminum foil and shlep it to summer camp on visiting day at their children's request.

Kugels have found favor beyond the Jewish community. African-American chef Mildred Council owns Mama Dip's, a soul food restaurant in Chapel Hill, North Carolina. Her menu includes smothered pork chops, chitlins and kugel. After she was introduced to kugel at an interfaith community dinner, she created her own versions. One has dried cranberries in it; she serves it at Christmastime with cranberry sauce on top.

Farther afield, you can find the Lithuanian kugelis, a hot, crusty kugel that includes potatoes, eggs, onions, milk and – gasp! – bacon. A version of this migrated to Switzerland where what they call kugel comes with herring on top.

Kugel expert Allan Nadler, a professor of Jewish Studies at Drew University, wants none of it. "No spinach or zucchini or sweet kugel for me," said Nadler, who grew up in Montreal. "Everything is a kugel these days. I grew up in a home where my grandparents were from Russia. We ate salt and pepper kugel and cut it up in the soup. Now that's kugel!"

⌢ 27 ⌣

Hey, What Are You Calling Fat?

On Sundays, the family used to gather at *Bubbe* and *Zayde's* house. While the aunts and uncles *kibitzed*, we kids would keep Bubbe company in the kitchen. We'd watch her make chicken soup from scratch. When it had cooled down, she would skim the fat off the broth and scoop the yellow goo into a jar.

Other times, she would take bits of chicken fat and skin, add onions, and simmer it on the stove. When the skin was brown and crackly, she'd pour off the fat and call out, "Come eat now! I made *gribenes.*" Our parents loved it. We were happier with chicken soup and a scoop of her rainbow sherbet.

We didn't know from *shmaltz* back then. We thought it had something to do with music because when Judy Garland was singing "Somewhere Over the Rainbow" on the radio, Uncle Harry said, "It's so shmaltzy."

We've since learned. Shmaltzy is an adjective meaning overly sentimental or gushingly sweet. It refers to art or music, not food. Shmaltz, the noun, is rendered chicken fat.

In the days before cholesterol was a concern and alternatives were invented, most Jewish cooks of Eastern European origin collected goose or chicken fat to use as shortening. They couldn't cook meat in butter (a dairy product) or in lard (made from pork) because both violated kashrut, the Jewish dietary laws. And unlike Jews who lived in Mediterranean countries, they didn't have access to olive oil.

Shmaltz was both practical and tasty. It was an essential ingredient in Old World Jewish cooking, adding its characteristic flavor to chopped liver, potato *kugel* and *kasha varnishkes*. Shmaltz was also *shmeered* on rye or pumpernickel.

When we grew up, our moms preferred margarine – usually Fleischmann's – because "margarine is healthier for you." These supermarket substitutes gave Jewish cooks a way to use nondairy, butter-like products in their meat dishes and still keep kosher.

Some moms also kept a tub of gooey white Crisco in the pantry. When Procter & Gamble introduced the "first solid shortening made entirely of vegetable oil" in 1911, they advertised it as "a product for which the Hebrew

Race had been waiting 4,000 years." Because it was made of vegetable oil, Crisco could replace butter or animal fat in recipes, and it was certified kosher. In 1933, P&G produced a bilingual Yiddish-English booklet of Crisco recipes for the Jewish housewife.

Years later we learned that margarine contained those bad-for-you trans fats and had the same calorie count as butter. So much for all those years of sacrifice: We could have been eating butter!

We do now – and not only Land O'Lakes salted and unsalted butter, but also pure Irish butter and butter made from the milk of New Zealand cows that graze on organic open pastures year-round. While we no longer buy margarine, we continue to buy other butter substitutes. We've used Smart Balance, a "natural oil blend," and a few of its "buttery spread" competitors. Crisco now comes in "butter-flavored" baking sticks that are yellow, not the strange bright white of old; these come in handy when we make chocolate chip cookies.

We also use cooking sprays – olive oil, butter-flavored, and the one with flour that works so well for baking. We no longer have to grease and flour the pan and tap the extra flour into the sink, but the spray might be a trade-off, considering the chemicals needed to propel it.

We're not nostalgic for the old days when cooks only had a choice between shmaltz and shmaltz, but other people are. Shmaltz is making a comeback. In *The Book of Schmaltz: Love Song to a Forgotten Fat,* culinary writer Michael Ruhlman asserts that shmaltz can be the star in recipes from fluffy gnocchi to oatmeal cookies. Modern chefs have taken notice of shmaltz's rich taste, and it's being served in fancy restaurants as a bread spread, added to ramen recipes, and used to cook french fries. It's only a matter of time before local delis start placing little jars of delicious, creamy, salty, artery-clogging shmaltz back on each table.

In the meantime, you can often find shmaltz in the kosher section of a supermarket or have it shipped from Schmaltz Deli in Naperville, Illinois. We're pals with the deli on Twitter because they like our style and we like their name, but if we ever get to visit, we have a feeling we'd pass on the shmaltz and go straight to the *rugelach*.

Bubbe
Knows Best

～ 28 ～

No, You Can't See My Knipple

Knipple sounds like a dirty word, like what you'd see if you peeked into the women's dressing room in a department store or what may accidently slip out when you're wearing a low-cut dress. But *knipple* is not a body part. It has nothing to do with bosoms.

A knipple (you pronounce the K) is a woman's secret stash of money. It means "a little piece you break off," wrote author Sissy Carpey in her memoir, *A Piece of Her Heart*. It's like when you're baking and you break off a knipple of dough to make a cookie, so it makes sense that a knipple is also a little bit of money liberated from a larger, shared joint bank account – a little bit of dough for yourself.

Before Sissy got married, her Aunt Yetta gave her some marriage advice, not about sex but about money: "Every woman needs her own knipple. No wife should have to ask permission from her husband to buy a dress for a family occasion, a gift for a child or a piece of jewelry," Yetta told her.

Liz Perle, author of *Money, A Memoir*, learned about knipples from her *bubbe*. "My grandmother went over to her pocketbook, a black patent leather rectangle with a silver clasp that I liked to snap open and shut. She took out a $20 bill, folded it twice and handed it to me. 'This is the beginning of your knipple,' she told me. 'Every woman needs money of her own that her husband never knows about so she can do what she wants. Remember that.'"

Even the wife of a king needs a knipple. In fact, the concept of a wife setting aside some money for her own use dates to 1540 when hairpins were imported from France for Catherine Howard, the fifth wife of Henry VIII. These pins were expensive, and husbands would give their wives a little extra money – pin money – to purchase them. Ironically, to get money today you need to remember your PIN, but that's a different kind of pin money.

Philadelphia real estate developer Henry G. Freeman thought that the wife of the President of the United States needed pin money, too. When he wrote his will in 1912, he established the Pin Money Fund for the First Ladies' "own and absolute use." Barbara Bush got $36,000 from the fund; she donated a portion to charity and used an unspecified amount to "do something nice for my grandchildren." Although her grandchildren don't call her Bubbe, she surely acted like one on that occasion.

If you don't have a palace or a big white house in which to hide your knipple, where would you put it? Knipple comes from the Yiddish word "knip," meaning pinch, which provides a clue: A bubbe would make a pinch or a knot in the fabric of her apron – no *balabusta* went without one – and tuck the cash inside. One *zayde* recalls that his wife would wear many aprons, one on top of the other. She would hide her money either in the pockets or in a knot she tied in the bottom apron. We hope she moved her knipple, because it wasn't such a secret after all!

These days, with aprons a thing of the past, knipples are being hidden anywhere a husband wouldn't think to look – in a box of tampons in a bathroom cabinet or in a canister on a pantry shelf. A knipple could be a roll of bills at the bottom of an underwear drawer or a $100 bill tucked into the inside pocket of a purse.

Ellen's mother has a knipple. She showed its hiding place to her daughters when they were teens and told them they should have a knipple of their own one day. Then she denied its existence and swore them to secrecy.

We don't have knipples. We both earn money on our own, and we don't have to ask our husbands before we send a care package to our college kids or buy something new to wear. But after all of this research, the idea of keeping $200 tucked away in our underwear drawer – just for us – sounds like a fine idea. Our bubbes would be proud.

Stirring Up
Chicken Soup Memories

Every grandmother has her favorite soup recipe. A nonna makes ribollita, the Tuscan white bean soup. An abuela's staple is chicken posole with chili powder and hominy; an awa likes to cook up moong dal, an Indian spiced lentil soup.

If you have a *bubbe*, chances are you have fond memories of chicken soup. "I lived for my bubbe's chicken soup," said our friend Jill. "I can still picture my grandmother in her kitchen stirring a big pot of soup. I had to stand on a stool to look into it." Her grandmother's soup had clear broth with no carrots or celery in sight, and as a little girl Jill got to choose whether bow ties, alphabets or thin egg noodles were added to the broth.

One friend attributes the rich yellow color of her bubbe's chicken soup to the chicken feet that were an essential part of her family's recipe. She loved that soup and wanted to make the recipe, but when she asked for chicken feet at the local supermarket, she was told to go to Chinatown. She did without.

Others recall trips to the kosher butcher to help their grandmother pick out just the right chicken. It came home with all its parts – the gizzard, heart and liver – which went right into the soup pot along with the feet. "I liked all the parts," recalls Joyce's husband, Ted, "but I loved the eggs the most. My mom would ask the butcher to be sure to include them."

Eggs? He was referring to *eyerlekh* (little eggs), the not-fully-developed eggs found inside a laying hen. He isn't the only one who raves about the firm yellow egg yolks floating in their grandmother's Friday night chicken soup: "They were like nothing else," one fan said. "Golden treasures," said another.

When it came to something floating in their soup, many people preferred *mandlen*, those puffy little round crackers. You may have called them "soup nuts."

But the highest praise was reserved for matzah balls. The Yiddish word is *knaidlach*, as in "Don't be stingy; give the boy more knaidlach." Just the mention of matzah balls can start a heated discussion about whether your grandmother's were sinkers (heavy and compact) or floaters (light and fluffy) and which you liked better.

The proper way to construct and cook a matzah ball has been the subject of Talmudic debate for hundreds of years. Do you add seltzer to the egg mix to make the balls lighter? Does boiling them first in plain water rob them of flavor? Should you cover the stockpot tightly and resist the urge to peek to ensure they are fluffy and thoroughly cooked?

While you won't find matzah balls anywhere other than in a bowl of soup, *kreplach* lead a double life. The stuffed dumplings that are similar to ravioli and wontons are equally at home in soup broth or on a plate topped with sour cream and fried onions.

Joyce is pleased to have her bubbe's vintage aluminum stockpot, which is so tall it doesn't fit in her kitchen cabinet, but she doesn't have her bubbe's chicken soup recipe. Bubbes rarely wrote down a recipe. They cooked from memory and by taste. When we would ask Bubbe for a recipe, she'd say, "You don't need a recipe. You just add a *bissel* of this and a *bissel* of that."

If we persisted and asked exactly how much salt to add, she'd say, "*Shitteryne!*" We thought she was cursing, but she was telling us to pour it in without measuring. When we asked a friend if she knew the word shitteryne, she told us, "My mother's aunt used to make shitteryne cookies." No use asking for the recipe for those.

When Bubbe did measure, she didn't depend on manufactured measuring cups; she used what she had in her kitchen. She'd wash out the patterned tumbler that Breakstone's sour cream came in or use the old glass from a yahrzeit memorial candle.

For generations, bubbes have been claiming that there's nothing like a bowl of chicken soup to cure a cold. Drinking the hot soup and breathing in the steam gives you nourishment and makes you feel better. It's called "Jewish penicillin," but chicken soup was prescribed for more than 800 years before penicillin was discovered. In the 12th century, Maimonides, the Jewish rabbi and physician, recommended the broth of hens and other fowl to "neutralize the body constitution." That's some endorsement for a bowl of chicken soup! Unfortunately, Maimonides didn't offer any advice on how to make knaidlach light and fluffy.

In a Jewish home, you don't need to be fighting a cold or sitting down to Shabbat dinner to get some chicken soup. Even on Thanksgiving, before the turkey and sweet potatoes are served, Jewish hostesses have been known to ask, "Do you want one matzah ball or two?"

⌒ 30 ⌒

Kine-ahora,
I'm as Healthy as a Horse

If you are superstitious, there are certain situations you'll want to avoid: Walking under a ladder. Breaking a mirror. Killing an albatross. A black cat crossing your path. But no matter how vigilant you are, it's hard to steer clear of the evil eye. It can be lurking anywhere.

The belief that a menacing glare can bring bad luck or inflict harm is common among many cultures. Look around any open-air marketplace in Brazil, Greece, Ethiopia or Israel and you'll see evil eye talismans being sold to ward off this curse.

The superstition is ancient, but it still maintains its fear factor. The evil eye is mentioned several times in the *Pirke Avot* (Ethics of the Fathers), a collection of quotes from Jewish sages and scholars. "An evil eye is worse than a bad friend, a bad neighbor or an evil heart," wrote Rabbi Eliezer, one of these scholars.

Bragging about one's good fortune could anger an envious human being or the random dybbuk, a wandering spirit that is waiting to cast its evil eye on you. That's why *bubbes* will warn you not to boast about your good health, good news or the accomplishments of your children. *Kvelling* that your daughter just got into medical school will only provoke the evil eye to get her expelled in her first semester. Blogger Miryam Ehrlich Williamson sums it up perfectly: "The evil eye smells kvelling the way a mouse smells cheese."

One way to counteract this jinx is to invoke the Yiddish phrase *kine-ahora*, the verbal equivalent of knocking on wood. Kine-ahora comes from the German "kein," meaning no, and the Hebrew "ayin ha-rah," meaning evil eye. You can use it when you share some good news, as in "My bad back hasn't bothered me lately, kine-ahora."

Likewise, you can ward off the evil eye when you are paid an extravagant compliment.

"You look stunning today, Sylvia. Is that a new dress?"

"I just got it, kine-ahora. Do you like it?"

When kine-ahora is said quickly, it can mutate into the Yinglish "canary." This is why someone might be heard to say, "I'm supposed to leave next Sunday for vacation, so don't give me a canary."

Instead of uttering "kine-ahora," you could spit three times to ward off the evil eye. Romans called this custom "despuere malum," to spit at evil. Since bubbes like to mind their manners, you are more likely to hear them saying "poo-poo-poo" as they pretend to spit, hoping the evil eye doesn't notice that they're faking.

When you need an extra dose of protection, you can go all out and say "kine-ahora, poo-poo-poo" and also adorn yourself with an evil eye talisman. Blue glass beads that resemble eyeballs come attached to silver necklaces, antique rings or pins that can be fastened onto a baby's onesie.

If an eyeball gives you the creeps, consider a hamsa, an amulet shaped like an open hand; it's a popular symbol in Middle Eastern culture. Hamsa comes from the Hebrew and Arabic word for five; the five fingers symbolize the protective hand of God and are thought to keep the wearer safe from the evil eye. Five also represents the Five Books of Moses.

It's no surprise that people who are superstitious are most anxious to protect the *kinder*. After all, who needs immunity from the evil eye more than a defenseless child? That's why when a bubbe is asked, "How many grandchildren do you have?" she may reply, "Kine-ahora, not seven." If the evil eye doesn't have an accurate kid count, there's less chance those children could be harmed.

Ashkenazic Jews traditionally avoid naming a baby after a living relative so that when the Angel of Death shows up he doesn't make a mistake and take the baby instead of the elderly family member. By naming a baby in honor of a deceased relative, preferably one who lived a long time, parents not only honor that person but also avoid all the confusion and keep their child safe from the evil eye.

Another way to keep the evil eye at bay is to refrain from purchasing baby clothes or setting up the nursery until the baby is born. If the evil eye should see you painting the nursery pink or setting up a crib, who knows what might happen?

In Israel, where they've adopted so many western customs, such as wearing white wedding dresses and eating fast-food hamburgers, it's still unheard of to hold a baby shower before the baby is born. In the United States, Jewish families usually arrive at some compromise, like storing the shower gifts at a parent's house or buying a crib but not assembling it until the baby has safely arrived. When a bubbe comes to visit for the first time, she'll likely insist that you tie a red ribbon to the crib, stroller, playpen and even the baby's underwear. The red ribbon makes the child imperfect, and the evil eye will stay away.

One man recalls that his mother made him chew on a piece of thread whenever she sewed a button back onto the shirt he was wearing. She, too, was trying to fool the Angel of Death: Jewish funeral custom dictates that a white linen shroud be sewn around the body of the deceased, so if the boy was moving his mouth while she was sewing, it was a sure sign that he was still alive and not ready for a shroud. Try explaining this to a child.

Did your mother ever tell you not to leave your dishes in the sink or your book open on the table? The first command is simply good housekeeping; the second one is an old superstition. If a prayerbook was left open on the table, clever devils or evil spirits who happened by could "read" the holy book, take the knowledge and use it to make trouble. That's why you should always close your book, even if you're reading Danielle Steel or Stephen King. Turn off your Kindle, too.

In ancient times, you could die from an infected tooth. An eclipse meant the world was ending. You could starve to death because there was no pizza delivery.

People tried anything to exert some influence over the mysterious workings of the universe, even if it meant spitting, saying kine-ahora and wearing an eyeball-shaped necklace.

Life can be tenuous today, too, so we wear our hamsa necklaces and carry our evil eye key chains to keep safe. It's like cooking up a big pot of chicken soup when our kids have a cold. It couldn't hurt.

Farmisht and Farblondjet but Not Yet Alter-Kackers

⌒ 31 ⌒

How'd We Get to Be This Old?

In our minds we are young, but the evidence is mounting that we are just fooling ourselves.

When we read the Class Notes in our college alumni magazine, we're surprised that our graduation year is way at the back with the "old guard" and the "venerable alums," not at the beginning of the list with those who graduated in this century.

When we fill out forms on the computer, we often have to click and scroll down – and down and down – until we find our birth year buried deep in the list. Our only solace is that one list went back as far as 1891. We can only hope that the folks born then are still clicking and scrolling on their computers.

Okay, we're not young, but we don't think of ourselves as old. We can't believe we graduated from high school so many decades ago and that those 55-plus communities are meant for us.

How should we describe ourselves? As "mature"? We don't always act mature. We aren't "elderly." That's our parents. Are we "older adults"? Maybe. We are older than our adult children. The word "seniors" brings to mind seniors in high school, which sounds like much more fun than the seniority we see looming on the horizon.

In Yiddish, a cute little girl is a *maideleh* and a sexy young woman is a *tchotchkeleh*. So what's the Yiddish word for women of our age? There's *alter-kacker*, a decidedly uncomplimentary and vulgar expression that means something like "old fart." We don't want to be alter-kackers. Then there's *bubbe*. We will definitely be happy with that title, but we're not there yet.

When people ask us our age, we find ourselves having to do the math, silently subtracting our birth year from the current year – after we remember what year it is. When our birthdays come around, we're forced to figure out our age repeatedly, but when the day is done we don't store the offending number in our memory bank for retrieval. We delete it.

Happily, it's rare to see our ages publicized these days, except occasionally on a birthday cake. So it was a surprise when we signed up for an art class and saw our names, followed by our ages, posted on the classroom door. Who needs a shock like that? Names, followed by ages, should be reserved for arrest warrants, obituaries and gossip columns: "Prince Albert II of Monaco, 52, will marry the willowy blonde Charlene Wittstock, 32."

This is why one of us asked that her husband's age be left off the giant Jumbotron scoreboard at the ballpark when his name was listed with all the other birthday boys and girls at the game. She knew he wouldn't want to see his age up in lights in front of 40,000 other fans. The scoreboard simply read "Happy Birthday." The fans were left to figure out if the birthday boy was hoping for a new PlayStation or a glass of prune juice.

Perhaps we can draw on gematria, the ancient system of Hebrew numerology, to disguise our ages. According to this system, every Hebrew letter is assigned a numerical value. For example, "chai," Hebrew for life, is spelled with a "het," which has a value of 8, and a "yud," which has a value of 10, giving chai the value of 18. Gifts are commonly given in multiples of $18 as a wish for a long life.

Using this system – and some fuzzy math – our average age would be 2.92 chai. Unfortunately, we won't fool anyone. It's similar to the sizing system at Chico's, where a woman's large is a size 3. We love it, but they didn't fool us. When we buy a flowy, flowered shirt to hide our bulges, we know we aren't really a size 3. It's like giving your weight in kilos and hoping no one else knows the metric system.

We're in that gray zone – and we don't just mean our hair. We're too old to hold up our fingers when someone asks how old we are, not to mention that no one has 40-plus fingers. We're too young to brag about our longevity.

There are some benefits to being our age. No one asks us if we've lined up a prestigious summer job. We don't have to change out of a *shmatte* to run an errand. We don't participate in the Neighborhood Fun Run anymore; we just make a donation.

When we find ourselves complaining about growing old, we consider the alternative and snap out of it. So pass us the hair dye, our reading glasses and *AARP* magazine. We're just happy to be here.

～ 32 ～

We're Shvitzing

We love spring, with its daffodils and blossoming cherry trees, but we know it's a sign that summer's heat and humidity are just around the bend. In June, brides aren't glowing – they're dripping – and grads are thinking about going naked under their robes because it's so hot. They are *shvitzing*, and so are we.

Shvitz is the Yiddish word for sweat. Shvitzing isn't perspiring or having a moist glow; it's sweating so much you need to reapply your deodorant or change your shirt before dinner.

In our *Dictionary of Jewish Words,* it's fitting that shvitz is the entry right above shwarma, the spicy meat that's roasted on a spit over an open flame. We feel like we're roasting, too, when it's 92 degrees in June. To tell you the truth, we are roasting year-round, no matter what the temperature is outside. For us, global warming is personal.

When the mercury rises, we meticulously follow tips from the American Red Cross to "slow down, avoid strenuous activities and drink plenty of fluids." For years we have ignored the directive from the local fire department to make a family emergency evacuation plan, but we have no problem preparing for a weather emergency by lounging on the sofa, drinking ice tea, and ordering takeout instead of cooking dinner.

The medical term for excessive sweating is hyperhidrosis. This isn't your husband when he comes in from jogging. It's 2 to 3 percent of the population who sweat all the time, no matter what the weather or the activity. People who suffer from a severe case of hyperhidrosis can be so sweaty that it's hard for them to shake hands, hold a fork or grip a banister. Yuck! Maybe George Carlin was thinking of these folks when he said, "Don't sweat the petty things and don't pet the sweaty things."

Other causes of excessive sweating include menopause, diabetes, hyperthyroidism and chronic arsenic toxicity. If someone is slowly poisoning you with arsenic, being sweaty is the least of your worries.

We have no problem gripping the banister, so we're suspicious that menopause, not hyperhidrosis, is the cause of our chronic sweating. Menopause is why we sit inches from an air conditioning vent. It's why you won't find us in a hot yoga class where the room is 105 degrees as students assume awkward poses. Not one of them is downward resting sofa.

It doesn't help that our husbands don't shvitz. In fact, they are always cold. They often keep their fleece or jacket on in the house. Through decades of marriage, we've managed to agree on where to take the kids on vacation, how much to spend on a new car, and whose parents we're going to visit on Thanksgiving, but we rarely agree on the air conditioner settings. Our husbands dominate the TV remote control – and the thermostat. And we know we're going to sweat.

For centuries, people have paid to sweat. Bathhouses are mentioned in the Talmud, and the ruins of a Roman bathhouse complex built by Herod were uncovered on Masada in Israel. Why should we pay to sweat when we do it so freely on our own?

The bathhouse, or *shivtz-bod* (sweat bath), was a popular gathering place in Eastern European towns. After all, people who didn't have indoor plumbing or running water needed a place to go to clean up. When Jews immigrated to America around the turn of the 20th century, they brought along the tradition of "taking a shvitz." Immigrant neighborhoods, such as New York's Lower East Side, once boasted many steamy shvitz-bods where men could *shmooze*, relax, work up a sweat, and even grab some dinner. A special part of the experience was getting a *plaitza*, a rubdown with an oak leaf broom soaked in hot, soapy water.

The modern equivalent of the shvitz-bod is the day spa, with its relaxing aromatherapy baths, steaming facials and hot stone massages. That's the kind of shvitzing we'd pay for.

～ 33 ～

It's Summertime and
We Need to Rent a Kid

When we were kids, summertime meant: "Go outside and play."

Hopping on our three-speed Schwinn bikes gave us freedom. There was no need for helmets and no stranger danger. We could ride to the drugstore and get a milkshake at the soda fountain. We could pedal to the playground where we would surely find a friend, swing on the swings and hang out till dark.

When we heard the jingle of the ice cream truck, we'd grab a few coins from our allowance and run outside to be first in line. We'd ask for the chocolate éclair or the cherry ice pop.

Our cousins lived nearby. Together we'd listen to the latest 45s, read *Mad* magazine and play Monopoly while the aunts and uncles sat around the dining room table smoking and playing pinochle. As the sun went down and the kids started to whine – "Are we ever going to have dinner?" – Uncle Sid would lumber outside, drag the grill to the patio, douse the coals with lighter fluid, and pull out a package of Hebrew National hot dogs.

On family trips to the Shore, we would race to the ocean while the adults unpacked the car. No sunscreen, no hats, no shoes. We'd sunburn and peel, sunburn and peel, throughout the summer. We couldn't wait to jump into the ocean, no matter what the temperature.

Then we got married and had children. Our kids gave us a reason to do some of our favorite things all over again.

We joined the community pool because we could sit on the edge and chat with the other moms from the neighborhood. The kids would jump in on arrival. We wouldn't take the plunge until they begged us to put our heads under the water so we could watch them do a handstand.

If the ice cream truck arrived right before dinnertime, we didn't deny our kids because we wanted ice cream, too. We'd stand in line with them, helping them decide between the chocolate éclair and the rainbow push-up pop. Then we'd ask if we could have a bite.

We brought our bikes out of the garage, filled the tires with air and bought a child seat for the back. This time around, we all wore helmets. When the kids graduated to two-wheelers, we taught them to stop at the stop signs and watch out for cars. We'd bike along the river or ride with them to the variety store to get a fresh bottle of bubbles or a new balsa wood glider.

When our children were young, we loved going to Sesame Place and Hersheypark. We'd put on a brave face and climb the stairs of the tall water slide to show the kids it wasn't scary. We enjoyed the Muppet musical stage show as much as they did. Closer to home at the children's museum, we'd help them wheel a mini shopping cart through the kid-sized grocery store and ring up the plastic play food. At the Franklin Institute Science Museum, we would lead the way down tight, dimly lit passageways through the chambers of the heart. We always boarded the huge indoor steam locomotive with the kids for the 15-foot ride.

We wanted our children to spend time with their cousins, but this involved coordinating calendars around summer camp schedules and family vacations. It required advance planning: We'd drive miles to each other's houses for a barbecue or plan field trips to a Phillies game, an amusement park or the beach so that we could all be together.

Now our children are grown. We don't have grandchildren yet. We have no excuse for childlike behavior, and we miss it.

When we hear the ice cream truck's song, we still get excited but we don't run outside. Instead, we open the freezer and pull out a Haagen-Dazs dixie cup. We use the teeny plastic spoon that's built into the lid. Eating ice cream this way makes us feel like kids again.

Now we have bicycles with comfy seats and 18 gears and we love them, but by the time we load them into the car and gather the water bottles, suntan lotion and bike helmets, we're exhausted. It doesn't help that when we're riding, our husbands constantly warn us – "Car! Car!" They aren't quite as annoying as those "professional cyclists" in head-to-toe spandex who zoom past and shout "On your left!"

At the beach, we wait until the ocean temperature is nice and warm before we wade in. We look out for jellyfish, stay where the lifeguard can see us, and reapply sunscreen with SPF 100 when we get out of the water.

We wanted to check out Philadelphia's new children's museum, but adults aren't welcome unless accompanied by a child, and we couldn't find one to rent. We didn't get into the building until years later when we attended a fundraiser in the carousel room, but we couldn't ride it. It was nighttime and it was turned off.

When the animated film *Minions* came out, we had to skip it. We didn't want to go alone to the movie theater. Then we felt out of the loop when we saw all the black and yellow backpacks with googly eyes and glasses in the stores. The next time our kids came home, we forced them to sit on the sofa and watch it with us on Netflix so we could see what all the fuss was about.

When a business trip took us to Orlando, we couldn't resist going to Universal Studios. It was no problem to wait in line for the Harry Potter and Spider-Man rides without children in tow, but when we climbed aboard the flying couch for the Cat in the Hat Ride, we felt as if we should show a photo of our kids to prove we weren't stalkers.

It's not that we're not having fun anymore; it's just grown-up fun. Perusing the list of specialty summer cocktails and ordering the lemonade vodka freeze is pretty darn fun. So is going to the movies any night of the week without having to hire a babysitter.

So, hey, ice cream man, please stop. There are two middle-aged ladies chasing your truck down the street.

⌒ 34 ⌒

(Often) **Lost & Found** (Sometimes)

These days, we find ourselves losing things. We lose a half-full mug of coffee when we are changing the sheets. We carry two sets of car keys in case we misplace one. At the ATM we have to remind ourselves to "take the bank card, take the bank card" before we walk away.

We're women of a certain age. We're confused, distracted and forgetful. It sounds better to us when we describe it with Yiddish adjectives: We're *farchadat, farblondjet* and *farmisht*.

We comfort ourselves with thoughts like this: We may have lost a mug, but history lost thousands of Israel-ites. After the death of King Solomon, when the Assyrians conquered Israel, the 10 northern tribes of Israel disappeared from biblical accounts. Our coffee cup showed up two days later in the linen closet, so how come it took thousands of years to find some of those Jews in Africa?

When we multitask, we can't keep track of the multis. That's why when we got a screwdriver from the basement, walked upstairs, checked our email, picked up the sneakers strewn in the hallway, and turned off the bathroom light, we found ourselves asking, "What did we need a screwdriver for?"

Our neighborhood is a minefield of people who think they know us. "Friends" greet us by name, ask about our children and say, "See you at the meeting next week." Who are these people? How do they know us? What meeting are we missing? Scientists predict that one day virtual reality contact lenses will allow us to identify the person in front of us. This will come in handy at future cocktail parties to help us know who to future-*shmooze* with.

Who was the funny Jewish actor married to Anne Bancroft? We don't recall, and we worry that forgetting people's names, losing car keys and misplacing cups of coffee are signs of aging. We were happy when we read recently that if you can remember what you forgot – even days later – it's not dementia.

Mel Brooks!

It's frustrating to lose things and embarrassing to admit that we forgot to meet you for lunch and couldn't find our cellphone to call you to apologize, so we've developed these strategies to cope with memory lapses and missing things.

We let it go and hope it will eventually turn up: We subscribe to the theory that lost items disappear to a huge pile somewhere and eventually just come back. If that's the case, our piles contain at least 19 socks, extra car keys and teaspoons. Perhaps when Queen Elsa sang "Let It Go" in the movie *Frozen*, she was simply hoping her white fur mitten that went missing in the snowstorm would come back from the pile.

We seek spiritual guidance: Catholics have a patron saint devoted to helping them find lost objects. St. Anthony, a Franciscan friar, first demonstrated his skill when he prayed for the return of a stolen book. Since then his fame has grown, and so has his portfolio of found objects. Italian grandmothers swear by the short rhyme: "Something's lost and can't be found/Please, St. Anthony, look around." These days, one group of Franciscan friars accepts prayer requests to St. Anthony via text message. We have their number stored in our phone.

We recently discovered that Judaism offers lost and found help, too, and the boss doesn't delegate the work to an associate. A prayer from the Book of Genesis asks God for assistance in finding a lost object: "All are presumed blind until The Holy One, blessed be He, enlightens their eyes." To reinforce the request, rabbis also encourage us to give tzedakah (make a charitable contribution). If all of the above fails, we might actually have to get up and look for the object.

We buy a new one: We can't go without our reading glasses, so when we lose a pair we buy a replacement, put it on the desk and then find the missing pair waiting there. Joseph should have heeded this advice when his brothers stole his coat of many colors. Even though he went on to fame and fortune in Egypt, he never replaced his favorite coat.

We have a theory that many of the items in a school's Lost and Found, such as the oversized pink sweatshirt with the glitter unicorn, end up there on purpose. The losers have no intention of finding them. We believe this because we've "lost" things, too. When an aunt came to dinner and asked why we weren't using the tiered, pressed glass cake stand she gave us in 1982, we lied and told her it was lost. We hope she doesn't know how to search for a replacement on eBay because she'll find thousands of "lost" ugly cake plates for sale there.

We take supplements and play brain games: We considered Ginkgo biloba, which is purported to cut down on memory loss, but we'd have to remember to take the pill. Instead we eat blueberry muffins because blueberry flavonoids are supposed to activate parts of the human brain that control memory. And we love muffins.

Experts also say that word puzzles keep the mind active. That's why we do the crossword puzzle in the newspaper every day. What's the answer to 4 across? A 5-letter word for "not misplaced."

Oh yeah. FOUND.

Glossary

alter-kacker n. (AHL-ter COCK-er) A vulgar expression literally meaning "old shitter," similar to the English expression "old fart." Used to describe a fussy, crotchety person or a dirty old man. Sometimes abbreviated as "A.K."

babka n. (BOB-kah) A loaf-like coffee cake made from a sweet yeast dough and swirled with cinnamon and/or chocolate. "If we're going to have coffee, you might as well slice me a piece of that *babka*, too."

balabusta n. (bah-leh-BOOS-teh) Literally, "mistress of the house." A complimentary term for a woman who can do it all, usually in reference to running a household. "She works full time and doesn't have any help, and she's still baking a cake and making treat bags for the party. She's quite a *balabusta*."

bashert adj. (bah-SHAIRT) **1.** Predestined or fated. Used when talking about two people who seem "made for each other," similar to the expression "a match made in heaven." *Bashert* can also refer to things that are a happy coincidence or seem fated. "I can't believe you happened to take this route home on the very day my car died. It's *bashert* that you showed up to offer me a ride." **2.** n. soul mate.

bissel n. (BISS-el) A little bit of something; a tiny piece. A cook might say she adds "a *bissel* of salt" to everything.

borscht n. (BOARsht) An Eastern European soup traditionally made with beets. *Borscht* is served cold, often with a dollop of sour cream on top.

bubbe n. (BUH-bee) Grandmother. The Yiddish equivalent of Nanna, Nonna or Grammy. Sometimes used as an affectionate term for any older woman. "Of course I'm bringing the kids toys and chocolate bars. I'm their bubbe."

bubbeleh n. (BUH-beh-leh) Literally, "little grandmother." A term of endearment for a woman of any age, similar to "darling" or "honey."

bubbe meise n. (BUH-beh MYE-suh) Literally, "grandmother's story." **1.** A superstition or old wives' tale. "My mother would always warn me about going out-doors with wet hair, but that's just a *bubbe meise*." **2.** Something of little importance, inconsequential. "Stop complaining about the splinter on your hand. It's a *bubbe meise*, not a real injury."

bubkes n. (BUP-kiss) Literally, "beans." Indicates some-thing that's worthless or that falls short of expectations. Sometimes used as a mild expletive. "I thought I'd get paid for watching their cat while they were on vacation, but when they came home they just said 'thank you.' I got *bubkes*."

bulvan n. (BULL-vahn) An ox or oaf; someone who is thick-skinned and thick-headed. A bulvan is physically strong but also coarse, boorish and unrefined.

chaloshes n. (khah-LUH-shess) A disgusting or horrible thing; in bad taste. Can refer to anything from a bad movie to a vile meal.

chazerai n. (khah-zeh-RYE) Anything of little value; junk. Cheap, worthless trinkets or souvenirs. "When the kids came home from the arcade, their pockets were filled with *chazerai*."

cholent n. (CHO-lent) A slow-cooked stew made of beef, beans and vegetables. *Cholent* is a common Sabbath dish because it can be prepared the day before and cooked overnight on a low flame that is lit before Shabbat, in accordance with the prohibition against kindling a flame on the Sabbath.

chutzpah n. (KHUTZ-pah) From the Hebrew word for "audacity." Nerve or gall. Gutsy, sometimes arrogant behavior that is outrageous but at the same time admirable.

draykop n. (DRAY-cup) Literally, "turn head." A nutty, illogical person; someone who twists and confuses things.

eyerlekh n. (AYE-er-leck) Literally "little eggs." The not-fully-developed eggs found inside a laying hen. Jewish cooks used to put these firm yellow egg yolks in their chicken soup as a treat.

eyngeshparter n. (AYN-guh-shpar-ter) A stubborn person; mule-like. Someone who cannot be convinced with logic.

fapitzed adj. (fah-PITZED) All dolled up; overdressed for the occasion. Used to describe someone who wears inappropriate fancy clothes or too much makeup and jewelry. "She came to our house for a barbecue wearing Prada sandals, a diamond bracelet and leather pants. She is always so *fapitzed*."

farbissen adj. (far-BISS-en) Bitter, obstinate, scrooge-like. **farbissener** n. masc. (far-BISS-en-er); **farbisseneh** fem. (far-BISS-en-eh) A mean, unpleasant person; a sourpuss.

farblondjet adj. (far-BLON-jit) Lost; having no idea where one is. "Between reading the directions and looking for the sign, I was so *farblondjet* that I got off the turnpike at the wrong exit."

farchadat adj. (far-CHAH-det) Confused, distracted, mixed up. "She's a little *farchadat* since her children upgraded her cellphone to the new model."

farfel n. (FAR-full) Small pieces of noodles, usually sautéed with butter or oil, mushrooms and onions. *Farfel* is served as a side dish like rice or couscous. On Passover, *farfel* is made with crumbled pieces of matzah; and matzah *farfel* is a key ingredient in stuffing, *kugels* and other foods.

farkakteh adj. (far-COCK-tuh) Lousy, messed up, ridiculous. *Farkakteh* is similar to "crappy." "If I don't balance my checkbook every month, it gets all *farkakteh*."

farklempt adj. (far-KLEMPT) Overcome with emotion; all choked up. Someone who is *farklempt* may describe the feeling as a spasm or tightening around the heart and be at a loss for words or on the verge of tears.

farmisht adj. (far-MISHT) A little mixed up; confused. "I was so *farmisht* that I put the chicken in the oven but never turned the oven on."

farshtinkener adj. (far-SHTINK-en-er) Stinking, rotten. Used as a strong term of derision for anything from a stupid idea to a spoiled fish fillet.

fleishig adj. (FLAY-shick) The general term for food in the meat category, according to the Jewish dietary laws of kashrut. This includes beef and poultry and any byproducts, such as chicken broth and beef and chicken fat. It also refers to the pots, dishes and utensils used for cooking, eating and serving meat products.

fumfeh v. (FUM-feh) To speak unclearly; to mumble or hesitate. "He's nervous about giving the toast to the bride and groom. I hope he doesn't *fumfeh* too much."

gefilte fish n. (guh-FILL-teh FISH) Literally "stuffed fish." Deboned, ground fish – usually some combination of carp, pike and/or whitefish – that is mixed with matzah meal, eggs and seasonings; shaped into small patties; and simmered in broth or water. Served cold with horseradish, *gefilte fish* is a traditional appetizer at many Jewish holiday meals.

geshmak adj. (guh-SHMACK) Very tasty, delicious. "She made that stuffed capon just right. It was *geshmak*."

gonif n. (GAH-niff) Literally, "thief." A shady character, someone with questionable motives; a rascal. "That *gonif* wanted $6,000 for that old car. He told me it was 'gently used' by an old lady."

gornisht n. (GORE-nisht) Nothing, zilch, zero. The word can be used to describe someone who has nothing – no money, no personality, etc. *Er hot gornisht* (He has nothing) is similar to the English phrase, "He's so poor he doesn't have two sticks to rub together."

goyish adj. (GOY-ish) In the manner or style of a non-Jewish person; like a goy. Used to describe something that would be unlike or unfamiliar to a Jewish person. "When she dressed her daughter in that plaid skirt and beret, it was cute but she looked so *goyish.*"

gribenes n. (GRIH-bin-ess) The fatty skin of a chicken or other fowl, cooked with onions and salt until it is browned and crispy. The Jewish version of cracklings.

grober yung n. (GRAW-ber YUNG) A coarse young man; a crude, boorish fellow.

haimish adj. (HAY-mish) Unpretentious, homey; from the German word for "home." *Haimish* implies someone or something that is informal, welcoming and puts you at ease. "Their Shabbat dinners are very *haimish*; don't worry about what to wear."

kamishbrodt n. (kah-MISH-broot) A dry, crunchy, double-baked cookie similar to Italian biscotti. *Kamishbrodt* is made by forming dough into a log, baking it, cutting it into small slices, and then baking the cookies. It's usually plain or dusted with cinnamon sugar. Also known as kamishbread, it is *mandelbrodt's* plainer cousin.

kasha varnishkes n. (KAH-shah VAR-nish-kahs) A side dish of cracked buckwheat (kasha) mixed with bow tie pasta (*varnishkes*). It's served hot, often with gravy. It is sold at many delis alongside the *knishes*, lox and olives.

keppe n. (KEH-pea) Head. An informal, anglicized variation of the Yiddish word *kop.* "If only he would lay his *keppe* down, he would fall asleep on the car ride home."

kibitz v. (KIB-its) **1.** To fool around, joke or make wisecracks, particularly while others are trying to work or to be serious. "Enough *kibitzing!* Will you get out of my office already? I have to finish this work." **2.** To give unsolicited but good-natured advice. The word was originally used to describe a spectator at a card game who would make comments and give advice. **kibitzer** n. One who *kibitzes*.

kichel n. (KICH-ull) **kichlach** pl. (KICH-lock) Literally "cookie." A small cookie traditionally made with unsweetened dough and many eggs, which make it puff up. *Kichlach* can be plain or sprinkled with sugar. Also called bow tie cookies because of their shape.

kinder n. (KIN-der) Children. "Playing with the *kinder* makes me feel young again."

kine-ahora int. (KIN-eh-HORE-ah) An expression said to ward off bad luck or the evil eye, which might be listening in when things are too good. It's the verbal equivalent of knocking on wood. "I've felt good all summer, *kine-ahora*." The English word "canary" is the slang contraction of *kine-ahora*.

kishka n. (KISH-kah) **1.** A casing stuffed with a savory mixture of meat, flour or matzah meal, onion and seasonings; the Jewish version of sausage. **2. kishkas** Slang for guts or intestines. "He was just fooling around, but his last punch got me in the *kishkas*."

knaidel n. (kuh-NAY-dull) **knaidlach** pl. (kuh-NAID-lock) A dumpling made of matzah meal and beaten eggs, usually served in chicken broth. Another name for matzah balls.

knipple n. (kuh-NIP-pull) Literally, "pinch" or "knot." A woman's secret stash of money, which was commonly tucked inside a knot that was tied in an apron.

knish n. (kuh-NISH) A pocket of dough filled with meat or vegetables. It's most commonly baked but sometimes fried and is served hot, often as a snack or appetizer. Common varieties include potato, spinach, kasha and liver. Similar to an Indian samosa or a Spanish empanada.

k'nocker n. (kuh-NOCK-er) A showoff. A big shot who is boastful and cocky.

krechz v. (KREKHTZ) To sigh, moan or grunt about a little ache, pain or minor discomfort. The sounds are often accompanied by *"oy."*

kreplach pl. n. (CREP-lock) Small, paper-thin dough wrappers stuffed with meat, cheese or vegetables. Kreplach can be fried and eaten like pierogies or boiled and served in soup like wontons. "I put *kreplach* in the chicken soup because he doesn't like matzah balls."

kugel n. (COO-gull) or (KEE-gull) A baked casserole made with eggs and other ingredients. It's usually cut into squares and served hot. A noodle *kugel* can be sweet, with fruit, raisins and cinnamon; or savory, with spinach, mushrooms and onions. A crispy potato *kugel* with onions is an old-time favorite. "Every Friday night, my grandmom made a noodle *kugel* to go with her brisket."

kuvid n. (KUH-vid) Honor or recognition. In a larger sense, it can refer to the reward, actual or spiritual, gained from doing a good deed.

kvell v. (KVELL) To be extraordinarily pleased or proud; to be delighted. From the German for "gush," *kvell* means to burst with pride, usually over the accomplishments of children or grandchildren. "He got such a good report card. You must be *kvelling*."

kvetch v. (KVETCH) To chronically complain or gripe to others over minor issues and exaggerated aches and pains. "Stop *kvetching* about your sore ankle like it's a broken leg." **kvetcher** n. One who *kvetches*.

landsman n. (LAHNDS-man) A person whose ancestors came from the same town or region as another; a compatriot. Also used more generally to describe a fellow Jew.

latke n. (LOT-kah) A fried pancake. The most common type is the potato *latke* traditionally eaten on Hanukkah. *Latkes* come in many varieties, including sweet potato, carrot and zucchini. On Passover, latkes are made from matzah meal.

lekakh n. (LECH-huck) Honey cake, traditionally served on Rosh Hashanah. The dark, moist spice cake is made with honey, eggs, cinnamon and often coffee.

luftmensch n. (LOOFT-mench). Literally "air man." A dreamer; someone with his head in the clouds. A *luftmensch* is optimistic with no good reason and has big goals but doesn't take action. "He took one screenwriting class and already that *luftmensch* thinks his play is going to Broadway."

macher n. (MAKH-er) From the German word for "maker" or "doer." A big wheel; an operator. Someone who can use his or her connections to make things happen. Also refers to someone who is active in an organization. "He just joined our synagogue and already he's a big *macher* in the Men's Club."

mama loshen n. (MAH-meh LAW-shen) Literally "mother tongue." Used to refer to the Yiddish language itself. In the late 19th and early 20th centuries in Central and Eastern European Jewish communities, Yiddish was the language of the home, marketplace and popular literature. Hebrew was the language of prayer.

mandelbrodt n. (MON-duhl-broot) Literally, "almond bread." A dry, crunchy, double-baked cookie similar to Italian biscotti. *Mandelbrodt* is made by forming dough into a log, baking it, cutting it into slices, and then baking the cookies. Each baker has his own variation; some substitute pecans or walnuts for the almonds and add bits of dried fruit or chocolate chips. Also known as mandelbread, it is *kamishbrodt's* fancier cousin.

mandlen n. (MOND-lynn) Literally, "almonds." Small, baked, cracker-like balls with hollow centers that are floated in soup. *Mandlen* can be store-bought; they are often called "soup nuts."

maven n. (MAY-vin) An expert or connoisseur; a specialist. A *maven* is someone who has a certain interest or considers him or herself to be a trusted expert in a particular field.

mechayeh n. (muh-KHAI-yuh) Literally, "resurrection." Something that brings you back to life. A feeling of pleasure, delight or relief. Usually refers to a physical pleasure, like loosening a necktie or taking off tight shoes. "After being dressed up all day for the wedding, it was a *mechayeh* to take off my high heels and change into sweatpants when I got home."

mensch n. (MENCH) Literally, "person." A caring, decent person – man or woman – who can be trusted to do the right thing. It refers in a larger sense to acting in an honorable, proper way. The term is bestowed as a compliment on someone who has done the right thing without asking for thanks or credit.

mieskeit n. (MEES-kite) Ugliness; an ugly person or thing. It can refer to someone or something that is unattractive or unpleasant.

milchig adj. (MILL-khick) The general term for food in the dairy category, according to the Jewish dietary laws of kashrut. This includes milk, cheese, ice cream and milk products that may contain whey. *Milchig* also refers to the pots, dishes and utensils used for cooking, eating and serving milk products.

mishegoss n. (mih-sheh-GOSS) Foolishness, nonsense, craziness. It refers to wasting time or effort on something not worthy. "Spending all that money on baseball cards? Such *mishegoss*. He already has hundreds."

mishpuchah n. (mish-PUH-khah) Literally, "family." The extended family; the whole clan. *Mishpuchah* includes relatives by blood and marriage and sometimes even close friends. The word conveys warmth and friendship. "If the cousins are coming, we may as well invite the whole *mishpuchah* to the seder this year."

nebbish n. (NEB-bish) A loser; an ineffectual, timid person. Used to describe someone you feel sorry for. "He went to a fancy restaurant, and they gave him the table right in front of the bathroom. He didn't say anything. What a *nebbish*!"

nosh v. (NOSH) **1.** To have a little snack between meals or to eat a little something before a meal is ready. "Dinner won't be ready for an hour. *Nosh* on the cheese and crackers." **2.** n. A snack; a small portion. "She always packs a *nosh* for the car ride."

nosherei pl. n. (NOH-sheh-rye) Food for snacking; often refers to the free samples on a deli or bakery counter.

nu int. (NOO) A word with numerous shades of meaning; similar to a grunt or a sigh. An expression of uncertainty or questioning that requires a response, similar to "So?" "Well?" or "Come on, tell me." "Didn't you have a blind date last night? Was it fabulous? *Nu?*"

nudnik n. (NUD-nik) Someone who persistently annoys or pesters another person. "That *nudnik* kept asking me questions during the movie!"

ongeblozzen adj. (un-geh-BLUH-zin) Sulky, pouty; a sourpuss. "We're not going out for pizza tonight. Stop acting so *ongeblozzen*."

ongepotchket adj. (un-geh-POTCH-kit) Thrown together, not matching. Also, disorganized or cluttered, when talking about a space rather than a person. "She went to school in the flannel pants she slept in and looked all *ongepotchket*."

oy int. (OY) Perhaps the most popular Yiddish expression, *oy* conveys dozens of emotions, from surprise, joy and relief to pain, fear and grief. Sometimes used as *oy oy oy*. Also common are *oy vay* (short for *oy vay iz mir*), meaning "Oh, woe is me," and *oy gevalt*, a cry for help similar to "Oh, my God!"

oysgemutshet adj. (OIS-guh-moo-cheh) All tired out, exhausted; worked to death. "I'm *oysgemutshet* after I run around all day doing errands."

pesachdik adj. (PAY-sah-dick) Acceptable to be eaten on Passover; a term for foods that do not contain bread, flour or other leavened products that are forbidden on Passover. "Are you sure those cookies are *pesachdik*? They look too good to be made with matzah meal."

pitseleh n. (PIT-sel-eh) **1.** A little bit; a small piece. **2.** A term of endearment for an infant.

plaitza n. (PLAY-tzah) Literally "back" or "shoulder." A *plaitza* is a massage that involves a rubdown with soap-covered oak leaves. It is done in the steam room of the *shvitz*, or bathhouse.

plotz v. (PLOTS) Literally, "to burst." To explode or collapse from excitement, joy or surprise. "I won a prize in the Sisterhood raffle. I never win anything! I could *plotz*!"

pulkes pl. n. (PULL-keys) Thighs. It usually refers to cute, chubby baby thighs but can also mean those belonging to poultry. "Give that big slice of white meat to the children. I'm happy to eat the *pulkes*."

punim n. (PUH-nim) Literally, "face." Often used in the expression *"shayna punim,"* which means "pretty face." "Look at the *punim* on that boy! Is he adorable or what?"

pupik n. (PUH-pick) Belly button or navel. Used in perhaps the most famous Yiddish curse of all: *"Zoll vaksen tsibiliss in zein pupik!"* (Onions should grow in his navel!)

pushke n. (PUSH-kuh) A small container with a coin slot used to collect money for a charitable organization. In days past, homemakers would keep a *pushke* on the kitchen windowsill and put in a few coins each Friday before the start of Shabbat.

putz n. Yiddish (PUHTS) Vulgar slang for penis. The term is most often used as an insult for someone who is not worthy of respect; worse than a jerk. "He dropped out of college and never finished, but his resume says he graduated in 1981. What a *putz!*"

rachmones n. (rakh-MUN-iss) Pity or empathy, but with a sympathetic rather than scornful tone. "He's been looking for a job for six months now. Have a little *rachmones* and see if you can get him an interview."

rugelach n. (RUG-eh-lakh) Bite-sized, crescent-shaped pastries made by rolling dough around a variety of fillings, such as cinnamon sugar, raisins and chopped nuts; apricot or raspberry preserves; or chocolate. *Rugelach* are usually made with a cream cheese-based dough. A cousin to *shnecken*.

sekhel n. (SEH-khul) Common sense; good judgment. Using one's noodle. "Don't walk home alone at night. Have some *sekhel* and call a cab."

shanda n. (SHAN-dah) Scandal, shame. "He has a beautiful wife and four children, and everyone knows he had an affair. It's a *shanda* for the family."

shav n. (SHAV) Sorrel- or spinach-based soup, usually served cold and topped with a dollop of sour cream. Not as popular as its pink cousin, *borscht*, which is made from beets.

shitteryne n. (SHIT-teh-rine) A little of this and a little of that. *Shitteryne* often refers to cooking by instinct and taste rather than from a recipe. "When I asked *Bubbe* if I could photocopy her kugel recipe, she told me she didn't have one; she cooks by *shitteryne*."

shlemiel n. (shlih-MEAL) A foolish, clumsy, pathetic person; an oaf. A born loser who is to be pitied. "Poor Herbie is such a *shlemiel*. Just when he thought all his school loans were paid off, the bank sent him a notice about the one he forgot."

shlep v. (SHLEP) **1.** To carry or lug. "He shlepped the heavy carton home from the store. **2.** To drag someone someplace they don't want to go. "She shlepped me to the mall on such a beautiful day. We didn't get even a breath of fresh air." **shlep** or **shlepper** n. A beggar or a worthless person, often an unkempt one.

shlimazel n. (shlih-MAH-zull) Someone born under an unlucky star. An inept, bungling person who suffers from bad luck. The difference between a *shlemiel* and a *shlimazel* is commonly explained by the phrase: "It's the *shlemiel* who spills soup on the *shlimazel*."

shlub n. (SHLUB) A slob; some who dresses sloppily. "He didn't even change out of his gym clothes before their date. No wonder she doesn't want to go out with that *shlub*."

shluff v. (SHLUFF) Literally, "sleep." "It's past 9 p.m.; it's time for you kids get into bed and *shluff*."

shlump n. (SHLUMP) A dull, colorless person. Also describes someone who is a slob.

shmaltz n. (SHMALTZ) Rendered chicken fat. Jewish cooks used to collect and save poultry fat to use as shortening in recipes and for frying foods because commercial lard isn't kosher. Shmaltz gives the characteristic flavor to chopped liver, potato kugel and other old-time Jewish dishes.

shmaltzy adj. (SHMALL-tsee) Overly sentimental or romantic; gushingly sweet. Usually refers to literature, art or music, as opposed to food. "That old song is so shmaltzy. How can you like it?"

shmatte n. (SHMAH-tah) Literally "rag." An old, worn piece of clothing. "We're going out to dinner, so change out of that *shmatte*."

shmeer n. (SHMEER) **1.** A dab or a spread of something, like cream cheese on a bagel. **2.** n. The whole package, the full amount. "His son needed a new computer, and he decided to splurge and get him the whole *shmeer* – a computer, printer and even a new desk." **3.** v. To smear or spread. "*Shmeer* some butter on a piece of challah for the baby, will you?" **4.** v. To bribe or "grease the palm." "My father-in-law told me I should *shmeer* the maitre d' to get a good table in the restaurant."

shmeggegge n. (shmuh-GEH-gee) An untalented loser; a whiner. A *shmeggegge* could be considered a cross between a *shlemiel* and a *shlimazel*.

shmendrick n. (SHMEN-drick) Someone of no importance; a pipsqueak. A youngster still "wet behind the ears." "He's only been with the company for one year. They would not choose a *shmendrick* like him to head up the division."

shmo n. (SHMOW) A jerk, patsy or fall guy. A shorter, nicer way of saying *shmuck*. "I waited an hour for her to show up. I felt like such a *shmo* standing outside the theater."

shmooze v. (SHMOOZE) To engage in friendly, gossipy conversation; to chat. "On the first day of school, all the moms hung around in the parking lot to s*hmooze*."

shmuck n. (SHMUCK) Vulgar term for penis. **1.** A derogatory term for a detestable or obnoxious person. Harsher and more insulting than *shmo* or *shnook*. **2.** Someone who allows himself to be taken advantage of; similar to "jerk" when used in a self-deprecating way. "I can't believe I loaned her money again; she never pays me back. I'm such a *shmuck* sometimes." *Shmeckel* is the diminutive.

shmunda n. (SHMOON-dah) The Yiddish slang for vagina. *Shmundie*, the diminutive, is the childish version of the word.

shmutz n. (SHMUTZ) Dirt, stain or filth. "Come here and let me wipe that *shmutz* off your face." adj. **shmutzig**.

shnecken n. (SHNEH-ken) Literally, "snail." Bite-sized pastries made by rolling dough around filling jelly-roll style. Individual pastries are then sliced from the log and baked. Varieties of *shnecken* include cinnamon, chocolate, raspberry and other fruits. A cousin to *rugelach*.

shnook n. (SHNOOK) A passive, unassertive person; a patsy. The term is affectionate, not derogatory. A *shnook* is deserving of pity but also likable.

shnorrer n. (SHNOR-er) A beggar or moocher; someone who borrows something with no intention of repaying. "He goes to Costco every Thursday just to eat the samples. What a *shnorrer!*"

shnoz n. (SHNOZ) Slang for nose. Usually refers to a large or unattractive proboscis. "She's a cute baby, but look at the *shnoz* on her. I hope she grows into it."

shpilkes n. (SHPILL-kiss) Literally "pins." Impatience, nervous energy, restlessness. Someone with *shpilkes* is fidgety and might be described as having "ants in his pants." "She had *shpilkes* while she was waiting to be called for her audition."

shtarker n. (SHTAR-ker) A strong, brave person; a tough guy. *Shtarker* can refer to physical strength or mental endurance, such as someone with a lot of patience.

shtetl n. (SHTET-ull) A little town or village, specifically the rural communities in Central and Eastern Europe where many Jews lived before World War II. These villages were the heart of Ashkenazic Jewish culture until the Holocaust wiped them out. *Shtetl* life was portrayed in the paintings of Marc Chagall, the stories of Sholem Aleichem and the musical *Fiddler on the Roof.*

shtick n. (SHTIK) Overused actions or behavior. A contrived gesture or attention-getting routine. "That comedian hasn't changed his *shtick* since 1982!"

shvitz v. (SHVITS) **1.** To sweat heavily. "Turn down the heat! I'm *shvitzing*." **2.** n. steam bath. Going to the *shvitz* was once a popular activity for Jewish men.

spiel n. (SHPEEL) A long, involved story or tale. It sometimes refers to a sales pitch or persuasive argument. "I made the mistake of telling him I was interested in buying a car. He gave me the whole spiel on why I should lease."

tchotchke n. (CHACH-kah) Literally, "doll." Any cute but insignificant object, such as a trinket or inexpensive souvenir. "I can't even dust the shelves anymore because they're filled with so many *tchotchkes* from our trips."

tsedrayte adj. (tsuh-DRATE) All mixed up, confused. "I had so much to do on Monday that I completely forgot to pick you up. I'm sorry I was so *tsedrayte*."

tsuris n. (TSORE-iss) Troubles and worries; problems. "Her older son is so irresponsible, and her husband is having troubles at work. So much *tsuris* in that family!"

tuchis n. (TUH-kiss) Literally "underneath." Vulgar term for the rear end or buttocks.

tummel n. (TUM-mel) Noise, commotion or disorder. "I can't hear you. The kids are running through the kitchen and making a *tummel*."

vilde chaya n. (VIL-dah KHI-yah) A wild animal or someone who behaves like one. "She shouldn't bring her daughter to the restaurant because the child runs around like a *vilde chaya*."

yachne n. (YOKH-neh) A gossip, a busybody. A coarse, loud-mouthed woman who carries tales.

yarmulke n. (YAH-mih-kah) The small, round head covering worn by Jews as a sign of reverence and religious observance. While some Jews wear a *yarmulke* all the time, others wear it only in synagogue. The Hebrew word is *kippah* (KEY-pah).

yenta n. (YEN-tah) A gossipy woman; a blabbermouth. Someone who can't keep a secret. "I wonder what Ethel's husband does for a living. I'll have to ask Sylvia; she'll know. She's such a *yenta*."

yichus n. (YICK-iss) Pedigree, lineage, family background. The term usually implies that someone comes from a distinguished family with status or prestige. *Yichus* comes with responsibility: You can't just depend on your status; you must demonstrate virtue and do your part to earn your *yichus*.

Yiddish n. (YID-ish) From the German *"juedisch,"* meaning Jewish. Yiddish, which is written with Hebrew characters, is a version of High German with words from Hebrew, Old French, Old Italian and some Slavic languages sprinkled in. Yiddish was widely spoken by the Jews of Eastern and Central Europe (Ashkenazim), many of whom emigrated from Germany and Bohemia. Yiddish is a colorful language that spawned a rich tradition of theater, music and literature at the end of the 19th and early 20th centuries. With the destruction of most of Europe's Jewish communities by the Nazis and the adoption of Hebrew as the official language of the State of Israel, Yiddish fell into declining use. Today, it is enjoying a revival.

Yiddishkeit n. (YID-ish-kite) The qualities that describe Jewishness; a feeling or flavor of Jewish traditions, culture, ethnicity or manners. The word, which has a positive connotation, can describe anything from the plays of Neil Simon to the act of endowing a library in memory of a grandfather.

yutz n. (YUTS) A fool; a stupid or clueless person. Yet another Yiddish word to describe a loser. "It was her birthday and I forgot to send her a card. I'm such a *yutz* sometimes."

zaftig adj. (ZOFF-tig) Literally "juicy." A full-bodied, voluptuous, well-rounded woman.

zayde n. (ZAY-duh or anglicized as ZAY-dee) Grandfather. The Yiddish equivalent of Pop-Pop or Grandpa. Sometimes used as an affectionate term for any grandfatherly older man.

Joyce Eisenberg served as editor of Special Sections for the *Jewish Exponent* newspaper for 15 years and has edited Holocaust memoirs and a series of kosher cookbooks. She is the co-author of *The Scoop On Breasts: A Plastic Surgeon Busts the Myths* and a longtime contributor to Fodor's travel guides.

Ellen Scolnic writes about parenting, travel and topics of Jewish interest. Her humorous essays and feature stories have appeared in newspapers including *The Philadelphia Inquirer, Parents Express, The Christian Science Monitor, Main Line Life, Washington Jewish Week* and more.

Together, Ellen and Joyce are **The Word Mavens**. They are the authors of the *Dictionary of Jewish Words (JPS 2001, 2006)*. They write about Jewish holidays, family life, food and more for *The Forward*, InterfaithFamily.com and Jewish newspapers across the country; their essays on current events are frequently seen on *The Philadelphia Inquirer* Commentary Page. They blog, tweet, and interact with their fans at TheWordMavens.com.

Terry LaBan's cartoons, illustrations and infographics have appeared in numerous publications. He's worked in the comic book industry as both artist and writer. He created the nationally syndicated daily comic strip "Edge City," which ran for 15 years. He lives outside Philadelphia with his wife, two kids and two cats. Connect with him online at CartoonImpact.com.